THE QUALITIES OF MOTHERING:

Maternal Deprivation Reassessed

Michael Rutter, M.D.

THE QUALITIES OF MOTHERING:

Maternal Deprivation Reassessed

Jason Aronson, New York

First United States Edition 1974

Originally published in England
   as a paperback entitled
   Maternal Deprivation Reassessed

Copyright © Michael Rutter, 1972

LC: 74-18731
ISBN: 0-87668-189-5

Contents

Editorial Foreword

More than twenty years ago John Bowlby began to publish the results of his research on maternal deprivation, considering both its short-term effects on the child, and long-term effects in the development of pathological or deviant personality. The work has had a remarkable influence. It has led to a considerable amount of experiment, in animals and humans; it has resulted in practical changes concerned with the hospitalization of children; it has affected psychological theorizing, and drawn attention to the need to explain the characteristics of the child's bond with his mother; and, as might be expected, it has given rise to strongly held attitudes, often polarized, regarding methods of rearing children. Bowlby's approach to the topic was influenced by a psychoanalytic background and also by the early work of the animal ethologists. Michael Rutter, on the other hand, has the approach of a 'hard-headed experimentalist'. Considering these differences it is remarkable that their conclusions have so much in common: but of course there are differences.

In this book, Michael Rutter reviews the research and the theorizing, surveying a large amount of published work. He confines himself to the short-term and long-term effects of maternal deprivation in childhood only, and analyses carefully the various kinds of deprivation, and what is meant by quality of mothering. From his analysis he finds it necessary to distinguish between a failure to make bonds of affection, and deprivation after such bonds have been made. He is also careful to distinguish between various kinds of deprivation.

As well as discussing separation and deprivation, Dr Rutter asks whether or not there is something special about the bond of affection with the mother, or mother substitute. He concludes that it may be stronger than other bonds, but not different in kind. However, there are adults who would say that irreconcilable grief, for them, would be the result of the death of one particular person, and one only. If Dr Rutter is right, it looks as though some people become increasingly 'monotropic' between childhood and adulthood. Possibly there are big differences between different children, in that some develop several bonds and others only one, even when given the choice. There is indeed already evidence suggesting this.

Dr Rutter brings to his task a disciplined mind, a great deal of practical experience, and an obvious warm concern for the welfare of children. Research continues. Its outcome will be of theoretical interest, but also of great practical importance for our future.

B.M.F.

Acknowledgements

The ideas expressed in this book have developed through the course of many discussions with colleagues and friends over the last few years and to all of them I express my thanks. I am particularly indebted to Robert Hinde who has done much to clarify my ideas on 'maternal deprivation' and whose rigorous constructive criticism of an earlier draft of the manuscript eliminated many inconsistencies and faults of logic. Those that remain are mine alone. Many of my thoughts stem from my research collaboration over the last ten years with Jack Tizard and Philip Graham, to both of whom I owe a great deal. Their detailed criticism of the manuscript led to many improvements. I also received much help from others who have read and commented on the text – M. Berger, L. Hersov, R. Maliphant, James and Joyce Robertson, Barbara Tizard, W. Yule and a number of other colleagues. The original stimulus came from the results of studies into the effects on children of separation experiences and marital discord. My thinking on 'maternal deprivation' was much influenced by discussions with my colleagues on this project, whom I thank. I am also grateful to the Association for the Aid of Crippled Children (New York) for a generous grant which made the research possible. Like all other writers on 'maternal deprivation', I am indebted to John Bowlby, whose books and papers first opened up the subject and whose work has done so much to provide a stimulus on this topic. I am also most grateful to him for his helpful comments on a paper which formed the basis of sections of the book. Finally, I would like to express my gratitude to Catherine Greenwood and June Rice for the care given in the preparation of the manuscript and for help in checking references and proofs.

1 Introduction

No area of controversy in psychology has given rise to such widely differing assertions as the topic of 'maternal deprivation'. Thus in 1951, Bowlby concluded that ' . . mother love in infancy and childhood is as important for mental health as are vitamins and proteins for physical health' In sharp contrast, Casler, reviewing the same field in 1968, concluded that '. . . the human organism does not need maternal love in order to function normally'. Or again, more recently, Bowlby (1969) has gone so far as to suggest that individuals suffering from any type of psychiatric disorder *always* show an impairment of the capacity for affectional bonding and that frequently it is a disturbance of bonding in childhood which has caused the later psychiatric disorder. He suggests that this view provides guidelines for the day-to-day management of psychiatric patients. Conversely, O'Connor and Franks (1960) judged that the maternal deprivation hypothesis has not been experimentally confirmed to a degree which would warrant its acceptance as a guide to action.

Despite severe methodological and other criticisms (Casler, 1961; O'Connor, 1956, 1968; Orlansky, 1949; Wootton, 1959; Yarrow, 1961), the concept of 'maternal deprivation' has gained very wide currency and it has been held to be the cause of conditions as diverse as mental subnormality, delinquency, depression, dwarfism, acute distress and affectionless psychopathy (Ainsworth, 1962; Bowlby, 1951). While it has been recognized that the experiences subsumed under 'maternal deprivation' are complex, there has been a tendency to regard both the experiences and the outcomes as a syndrome which can be discussed as a whole (Jessor and Richardson, 1968). That different types of deprivation (perceptual, social, biological and psychological) tend to accompany one another is certainly true. However, as Yarrow (1961) emphasized, little progress is likely to occur until the basic variables indiscriminately combined under the term 'maternal deprivation' are differentiated and the separate effects of each determined. His thoughtful review suggested that different psychological mechanisms may account for different types of outcome. The present book seeks to explore this possibility in the light of the available evidence from research. No attempt will be made to criticize defects of design in individual studies, as this has been done in several previous reviews (see references above). Readers are referred to these and to other summaries of findings (Clarke, 1968; Dinnage and Pringle, 1967a, 1967b; Thompson and Grusec, 1970; Yarrow, 1964) to appraise the strengths and weaknesses of the raw material upon which this discussion is based. Rather, the data will be discussed in terms of their implications for concepts of deprivation, and deficiencies of the work will be touched on only very briefly when this is necessary to make sense of the findings. There is one further restriction in coverage – outcome will be considered only in terms of childhood and no reference will be made to the associations between childhood experiences and adult psychiatric disorder.

It will be appreciated that most psychiatric disorders have multiple causes. Quite apart from the effects of different types of 'maternal deprivation', there is good evidence that hereditary factors and organic damage or dysfunction of the brain play an important part in the genesis of emotional and behavioural disorders (see e.g. Rutter, Graham and Yule, 1970). The question of the relative influence of genetic, biological and psychosocial factors in particular psychiatric disorders will not be considered here. Rather, *within* that part of the variance which can be attributed to 'maternal deprivation', attention will be directed to which psychological mechanisms are concerned.

The material is organized in three parts. The first deals with the qualities of mothering considered necessary for normal development, the second with the short-term effects of 'deprivation' and the third with long-term consequences.

2 Qualities of Mothering Needed for Normal Development

Any discussion of mothering must rely heavily on Bowlby's writings, as his contributions over the last twenty years, ranging from his World Health Organization monograph in 1951 to his very important account of attachment behaviour in 1969, have been by far and away the most influential on this topic. In 1951 he stated that it was essential for mental health that the infant and young child should experience a warm, intimate and continuous relationship with his mother. He laid particular stress on the need for continuity and was explicit that this could not be provided by a roster. Nevertheless, while Bowlby (1969), in pointing to the importance of the mother–child *bond*, still regards an attachment to *one* mother-figure as crucial, he has always been explicit that 'it is an excellent plan to accustom babies and small children to being cared for now and then by someone else' (Bowlby, 1958b). Only in this way can mothers have the freedom to have some time released from child care to shop in peace or be with friends. He emphasized that particular care needs to be taken to ensure that alternative arrangements for mothering have regularity and continuity if mother goes out to work, but given this it may work out all right.

On the other hand, Bowlby's writings have often been misinterpreted and wrongly used to support the notion that only twenty-four hours' care day in and day out, by the same person, is good enough. Thus, it has been claimed that proper mothering is only possible if the mother does not go out to work (Baers, 1954) and that the use of day nurseries and crèches has a particularly serious and permanent deleterious effect (WHO Expert Committee on Mental Health, 1951).

The importance of a stimulating interaction with the child

has been emphasized by others (e.g. Casler, 1961, 1968). To these workers mothering consists of the supply of 'essential' stimuli which must be discriminable, functional and provide effective contingencies with the child's behaviour (Gewirtz, 1968, 1969).

Putting together these and other statements in the literature, six characteristics have usually been said to be necessary for adequate mothering: a loving relationship, which leads to attachment, which is unbroken, which provides adequate stimulation, in which the mothering is provided by one person, and which occurs in the child's own family. The evidence for each will be considered in turn in order to establish which features of 'mothering' appear important for development and which might be affected by 'deprivation'. The effects of 'deprivation' will be discussed in later chapters.

A loving relationship

'Love' is difficult to define and many writers have rejected this aspect of mothering as introducing mystical and immeasurable elements. However, characteristics of interpersonal interaction, as covered by terms such as 'warmth', 'hostility' and the like, have been shown to be susceptible to reliable measurement which can predict how family members will behave towards one another in other situations (Brown and Rutter, 1966; Rutter and Brown, 1966). In fact, the quality of family relationships has been found to be strongly associated with the nature of the child's psychological development in both cross-sectional and longitudinal studies (Craig and Glick, 1965; McCord and McCord, 1959; Rutter, 1971a; Tait and Hodges, 1962; West, 1969). Where warmth in the family is lacking, the child is more likely to develop deviant behaviour, particularly of an antisocial type. Thus, there is a good prima facie case for regarding 'love' as a necessary part of mothering. It should be added that the same evidence suggests that warmth is an equally important factor in parent–parent and father–child relationships with respect to their influence on children's development. This implies that, while warmth is a necessary part of mothering, it is not specific to mothering. Rather, it appears that warmth is a vital element in all kinds of family (and perhaps also extrafamilial) relationships. That warmth between parents (as well as between parent and child) may also influence the child suggests that it is not only as a factor leading to parent–child attachment that 'love' is important.

Attachment

There is good evidence that most children develop strong attachments to their parents (Ainsworth, 1963, 1964; Schaffer and Emerson, 1964). In his extensive review of the topic, Bowlby (1969) points to the universal occurrence of attachment behaviour in both man and subhuman primates. It may be accepted that this is a fundamental characteristic of the mother–child relationship. However, it is equally clear that there is great individual variation in the strength and distribution of attachments; the main bond is not always with the mother and bonds are often multiple. Thus, Schaffer and Emerson (1964) found that the sole principal attachment was to the mother in only half of the eighteen-month-old children they studied and in nearly a third of cases the main attachment was to the father. Although there was usually one particularly strong attachment, the majority of the children showed multiple attachments of varying intensity. It may be concluded that attachment is an important, perhaps crucial, aspect of the mother–child relationship, but equally it is a characteristic shared with other relationships.

Bowlby (1969) has argued that there is a bias for a child to attach himself especially to *one* figure (a characteristic he has called 'monotropy') and that this main attachment differs in kind from attachments to other subsidiary figures. However, there is a lack of supporting evidence for this claim; Schaffer (1971) has concluded that Bowlby's view is not borne out by the facts and that the breadth of attachments is largely determined by the social setting. The issue remains unsettled and requires further study.

If it is accepted that attachments are an important feature, it is necessary to proceed to the issue of what circumstances are required for their development. This is a question on which there are few facts in spite of an abundance of theories (Ainsworth, 1969; Bowlby, 1969; Cairns, 1966b; Gewirtz, 1969; Maccoby and Masters, 1970; Walters and Parke, 1965). The available evidence has been well reviewed by both Bowlby (1969) and Schaffer (1971). In this connection it is evident that proximity seeking and attachment to *specific* figures must be differentiated from dependency and attention-getting as a *general* characteristic. Bond formation is only concerned with the former (although non-specific attachment behaviour can lead to specific attachments).

If specific attachments are to develop with respect to individual persons it appears, although evidence on the point is lacking, that the *same* person must have contact with the child over a prolonged period on the grounds that attachments take time to develop. At least above a certain level, the absolute amount of time spent in the company of the child does not seem to affect the development of attachment, but the *intensity* of the parental interaction with the child probably is important (Schaffer and Emerson, 1964). Mothers who play with their child and give him a great deal of attention have a more strongly attached child than those who interact with the child only when giving routine care. Similarly, when a relatively unstimulating mother is found in conjunction with an extremely attentive father, the latter is likely to head the infant's hierarchy of attachment objects, despite the mother's greater availability (Schaffer, 1971). That intensity, rather than duration of interaction, is the crucial feature, is also suggested by anecdotal studies of kibbutzim children (Bowlby, 1969), who seem to be more often attached to their mothers (whom they see for short periods of intensive interaction) than to the metapelet who cares for them all day (but less intensively and as one of several children).

Schaffer and Emerson (1964) also showed that maternal responsiveness was associated with the strength of attachments. In cases where mothers responded regularly and quickly whenever their infants cried, attachments were strongest. Ainsworth (Ainsworth and Bell, 1969; Ainsworth and Wittig, 1969), on the basis of her observations of mother–infant interaction, also concluded that a key feature was the mother's sensitivity to her baby's signals. Attachments probably develop most readily to persons who can adapt their behaviour to the specific requirements of the individual infant, by taking into account the infant's individuality and by learning to recognize his particular signals (Schaffer, 1971).

Anxiety and fear, as well as illness and fatigue, tend to increase attachment behaviour (Bowlby, 1969; Maccoby and Masters, 1970). How this influences bond formation remains uncertain but it is probable that bonds are most likely to develop to the familiar person who is present, and so able to provide comfort, at times of distress. When a person is associated with relief of anxiety, an attachment is fostered. Whether the person is associated with anxiety or relief of anxiety obviously will depend on the circumstances. Children do not usually become attached to the dental nurse or the family doctor who gives them injections! Yet, under some conditions, they may actually develop attachments to people or objects who cause them distress. This has been shown experimentally in animals (Bowlby, 1969), but clinical experience suggests that the same may occur in man. Occasional parental rejection may actually increase attachment behaviour (in spite of the bond being less secure). It is parental apathy and lack of response which appear more important as inhibitors of the child's attachment.

The number of caretakers does not seem to be a major variable if other factors are held constant, but there is some suggestion that attachments may be stronger when the child has few caretakers (Caldwell, 1962; Schaffer and Emerson, 1964).

The content of the interaction appears largely irrelevant, and neither feeding nor caretaking are essential features – though they may facilitate the development of attachments (Schaffer, 1971). Attachments may develop to brothers or sisters (Schaffer and Emerson, 1964), and the presence of a child's even very young sibs may serve to reduce his anxiety in stress situations (Heinicke and Westheimer, 1965). Attachments may be formed to individuals who play with the child but do not feed him, and Schaffer and Emerson (1964) found that a third of children were mainly attached to someone who was *not* their principal caretaker.

It is uncertain whether the factors that aid attachment in animals are similar to those in man, but it seems that to the rhesus monkey body-contact comfort is more important than feeding (Harlow and Zimmermann, 1959) and that the type of surface contacted is relevant (Furchner and Harlow, 1969). However, if 'comfort' is held constant, both in that species (Harlow, 1961) and in dogs (Igel and Calvin, 1960), a lactating surrogate is preferred to one which is non-lactating. Little is known about the effects of facial appearance. However, a preliminary study (Gardner and Gardner, 1970) on just two monkeys suggested that this may also influence monkey preferences for different surrogates – although it is clear that this is at most a very subsidiary factor. Cairns (1966a, 1966b) reported that lambs can form attachments to animals they can see (through a glass panel) but not contact, showing that direct interaction is not essential. Mason's work (1968) implies that moving dummies may be preferable to stationary devices. All these experiments are useful in pointing to possible factors which may influence the development of attachments. However, it is clear from long-term studies of the rhesus monkey that, in spite of inducing attachments, surrogates of all types are almost totally ineffective as mothers so far as preventing the ill-effects of isolation is concerned (Harlow and Harlow, 1969, 1970). They provide immediate comfort in frightening situations, but in the long-term they are only marginally better than no surrogate and are very much worse than a monkey mother. Mothering requires a *reciprocal* interaction and so consists of far more than the passive reception of attachment behaviour (see accounts of the development of maternal behaviour in different species in Rheingold, 1963). This is well shown by Hinde and Spencer-Booth's (1971a) recent analysis of the dynamics of the developing mother–infant relationship in group-reared rhesus monkeys. It is also illustrated by the differences in mother–infant interaction in group- and cage-reared animals (Hinde and Spencer-Booth, 1967; Wolfheim, Jensen and Bobbitt, 1970).

In humans, there are variables not present in subhuman primates which also play a part. Language is the most important of these. This is influential both as a means of conveying feelings and emotions and through its role in thought processes enabling the infant to retain a concept of the mother when she is away from him. As well as factors directly concerned with mother–infant interaction, human studies suggest that the total amount of social stimulation provided may also influence the propensity to form attachments (although this possibility requires further study). Rheingold (1956) showed that extra mothering of six-month-old institutionalized infants led to an increase in their social responsiveness. Also, Schaffer (1963), in a comparison cf infants in hospital with those in a baby home, found that the first group (which had received less social stimulation) were slower to form attachments on their return home.

It should be added that the infants' own characteristics influence the development of attachment behaviour (Schaffer and Emerson, 1964), as they do other aspects of the mother–infant relationship (Bell, 1971; Harper, 1971). Moss (1967) found sex differences in early interaction; Prechtl (1963) and Ucko (1965) have shown how damage arising in the womb or soon after birth can influence the child's behaviour in ways that may influence the mother's response to him; and Freedman (1965) showed a genetic component in infants' early social responses. The behaviour of a neonate helps shape the response of his mother during feeding (Bell, 1964; Levy, 1958), and Yarrow (1963) showed that foster parents were influenced in their behaviour by the characteristics of their foster children. The child's contribution to parent–child interaction is a most important but much neglected subject.

The development of bonds in man has often been likened to the acquisition of a following response in nidifugous birds – a process known as 'imprinting'. Imprinting was originally regarded as a unique phenomenon which could develop only during a very short critical period in early infancy and which was irreversible once it had developed (Lorenz, 1935). Accordingly, it was once thought that the development of human attachments, too, might be restricted to a very narrow age period. It is now quite clear that this early view of imprinting was incorrect. There is no reason for thinking that imprinting is fundamentally different from other forms of learning; the period of its acquisition is influenced by environmental circumstances and is not rigidly fixed, and the following response is not irreversible (Bateson, 1966; Hinde, 1970). Nevertheless, the phenomenon is an important and interesting one and it remains true that it can only develop during a 'sensitive' period in early infancy (although this period is less clearly defined than first thought). To what extent the development of a mother–infant attachment in humans is similarly restricted to a particular phase of development remains quite uncertain (Schaffer, 1971). Undoubtedly, attachments can develop up to the age of one year (Schaffer, 1963) and often up to two years (Tizard and Tizard, 1972), but it is not known how long the readiness to develop an attachment can be maintained or what environmental circumstances are necessary for the readiness to persist. It is also quite unknown whether an attachment that develops late is as strong, stable and secure as one that develops early (Bowlby, 1969). These are important questions but ones to which no answers are yet available.

An unbroken relationship

The main reasons for regarding continuity as an essential requisite of mothering are the well-established associations between 'broken homes' and delinquency (see page 63), and the short-term disturbance which often follows a young child's separation from his parents (Yarrow, 1964). Both of these findings suggest that breaks in the parent–child relationship *may* have adverse effects, but as breaks are frequently associated with other adverse factors it remains to be established whether it is the separation as such which is the deleterious influence (this issue is discussed further in later chapters).

That transient separations are not necessarily a bad thing is evident from the high rate of separations in normal individduals. Douglas, Ross and Simpson (1968), in a national sample of some five thousand children, showed that by four and a half years of age, a third of children had been separated from their mother for at least one week. Furthermore, they showed that there was only a weak association between brief separations and delinquency (41 per cent separations in delinquents as against 32 per cent in controls). Of course, all children must separate from their parents sometime if they are to develop independent personalities, so the question is not *whether* children should separate from their mothers but rather *when* and *how* separations should occur. The finding that certain sorts of happy separation may actually protect young children from the adverse effects of later stressful separation (Stacey, Dearden, Pill and Robinson, 1970) also emphasizes the importance of considering the circumstances of a separation when deciding whether it is likely to be beneficial or harmful.

Perhaps an even more crucial point is the equation of 'separation' with 'discontinuity' in a relationship. In his 1951 monograph, Bowlby argued that the young pre-school child is unable to maintain a relationship with a person in their absence and that for this reason even brief separations disrupt a relationship. Experience with normal children suggests that this is not always so, at least in favourable circumstances. Of course, young children do find it more difficult, but it seems probable that environmental conditions as well as age influence a child's ability to maintain a bond during a person's absence. As the point is vital to the whole argument on continuity it deserves greater attention than it has received. The implications are discussed further in later chapters.

A 'stimulating' interaction

Different writers have varied greatly in the emphasis placed on 'stimulation' in mothering and on perceptual lack in 'maternal deprivation'. Some (e.g. Casler, 1968) have considered perceptual factors the most important influence, whereas others (e.g. Ainsworth, 1962) have regarded them as of only minor significance. Institutions have been used in many studies as an example of a deprivation situation and it is clear from several independent investigations that the sheer amount of adult–child interaction is one of the biggest differences between institutions and families (David and Appell, 1961; King, Raynes and Tizard, 1971; Provence and Lipton, 1962; Rheingold, 1960). On this basis it would be reasonable to include 'stimulation' as one of the hypothesized necessary elements in mothering, particularly as there is evidence that this is a necessary element in the development of language and intelligence (Haywood, 1967; Rutter and Mittler, 1972). However, it should be noted that 'stimulation' is a most unsatisfactory blanket term which means little unless further defined. Furthermore, although institutions may lack certain forms of stimulation, they differ from normal family life in many complex ways and it remains to be determined which differences lead to which effects. These issues are considered in more detail in chapters 4 and 5.

Relationship with one person

The suggested requirement that the mothering should be provided by one person is more controversial and not one given much emphasis by Bowlby (1951) in his WHO report. Although he expressed reservations about kibbutzim where mothering is shared between parents and metapelet (p.43), he suggested (p. 72) that large multiple-generation family groups had certain advantages in that there were always relatives at hand to take over the maternal role in an emergency. On the other hand, he has always (Bowlby, 1969) laid great emphasis on the hypothesized need for a child to attach himself specifically to just *one* person. Presumably if 'multiple mothering' did not allow this a child would be expected to suffer.

Actually there are several quite different situations included under 'multiple mothering', as Ainsworth (1962) has pointed out. First, there is the case where one major mother-figure shares mothering with a variety of mother-surrogates. This is exemplified by what happens when the mother goes out to work and in this situation there is good evidence that the children do not suffer provided stable relationships and good care are provided by the mother-surrogates (Rutter, 1971a; Yudkin and Holme, 1963). Secondly, there is the dispersal of responsibility among several (but not many) figures who have a high degree of continuity, as in the Israeli kibbutzim (Miller, 1969) or in societies with extended family systems (Mead, 1962). Again, although the evidence is quite weak, there is no reason to suppose that children suffer from this arrangement. Thirdly, multiple mothering may be associated with discontinuity and/or inadequate interaction, as in many long-stay institutions or residential nurseries. It is in these circumstances that children may suffer. While it is true that the number of mother-figures in institutions (sometimes a hundred plus) is usually also very much larger than is the case with either working mothers or kibbutzim, in practice a very large number of mother-figures virtually never occurs without there also being either discontinuity of relationships or inadequate interaction. It may be concluded that it is *not* necessary for mothering to be provided by only one person. In practice there is a strong tendency for situations involving very many mother-figures to be unsatisfactory in many other ways. Nevertheless, the very limited available evidence suggests that, if the mothering is of high quality and is provided by figures who remain the same during the child's early life, then (at least up to four or five mother-figures) multiple mothering need have no adverse effects. As this point is very pertinent to Bowlby's views on 'monotropy', well-controlled systematic studies are much needed to confirm or refute this very tentative conclusion.

Mothering in the child's own home

Finally, it has been suggested that mothering must be provided in the child's own home. Thus, Bowlby in his 1951 monograph maintained that children thrive better in bad homes than in good institutions and that a residential nursery cannot provide a satisfactory emotional environment for infants and young children. His more recent writings have shown that he is well aware of the complexities of the situation and of the dangers of comparisons of this sort. Nevertheless his early dictum was widely accepted and led to a very marked reluctance by some Children's Officers to remove children from even appalling home circumstances. It also led to foster homes being preferred as a placement over children's homes in spite of the fact that discontinuity of mothering is often just as great in foster homes (Dinnage and Pringle, 1967a, 1967b). Actually, there is no satisfactory evidence in support of the dictum 'better a bad family than a good institution'. Taken at its face value it seems to imply some mystical quality present in the family and suggests that the quality of mothering provided is irrelevant. This is such an obvious nonsense (and certainly not intended by Bowlby) that it scarcely warrants serious consideration. The development of children is so bad in the worst families – such as those where baby battering occurs (Helfer and Kempe, 1968; Skinner and Castle, 1969), where there is chronic discord and lack of affection between two psychopathic parents (Rutter, 1971a), or where parental social adjustment is at its worst (West, 1969), that even an institutional upbringing may be preferable. The outcome for children reared in institutions is certainly worse than that of the general population (Ferguson, 1966), but the outcome for many children from the best institutions is reasonably satisfactory (Conway, 1957; Tizard, Cooperman, Joseph and Tizard, 1972). The frequency of deviant behaviour in institutional children is well above population norms (Yule and Raynes, 1972), but equally it is below that of children in the most disturbed and loveless homes (Rutter, 1971a). The generally good adjustment of kibbutzim children (noted above) who sleep and spend their day in an institution (although remaining in contact with their parents) also argues against the suggestion that mothering must take place in the child's own home.

Nevertheless, there is something in the dictum in that it is clear that the quality and amount of maternal care provided in the *average* institution is much worse than the *average* family. Furthermore, the care in even the best institutions often falls well short of the average home although it is superior to the worst homes. As Bowlby (1951) rightly noted, it does seem peculiarly difficult for an institution to provide parental care of the quality and quantity expected in a family setting. The observation undoubtedly means that the greatest caution should be exercised in placing a child in long-term institutional care, but equally a bad home should not be automatically preferred to a good institution. It is necessary in each case to examine the quality of parental care provided (including its stability).

Other features

In the discussion up to this point, attention has been focused on those aspects of the relationship which have been emphasized in the scientific literature as supposedly specific to mothering. However, it is important to note that mothers fulfil many roles in the family and have an important influence on their children's development in a myriad of ways not so far discussed.

Obviously, the young child needs care and protection to ensure that he comes to no harm. As he grows older discipline and guidance are necessary. Food is essential to life and when young the infant cannot feed himself. In all these circumstances the mother is often a dominant influence in the home. Throughout childhood and adolescence both parents constitute models of behaviour for the child to follow (or reject). Play has a crucial function in psychological development (Millar, 1968) and although much play is with other children, play with parents is also influential in many ways. Some of the class-related differences between parents in their view of the use of toys may be important for children's later development (Bernstein and Young, 1967). Especially following Bernstein's theoretical papers (1961, 1965), people have become increasingly aware of the influence of parent–child communication on cognitive development, with particular respect to language functions (e.g. Bernstein, 1972; Hess and Shipman, 1967; Lawton, 1968). In all these (and other) different respects, parents are important. To what extent these variables determine the effects of 'maternal deprivation' will be considered in later chapters.

Conclusions

Mothering is a rather general term which includes a wide range of activities. Love, the development of enduring bonds, a stable but not necessarily unbroken relationship, and a 'stimulating' interaction are all necessary qualities, but there are many more. Children also need food, care and protection, discipline, models of behaviour, play and conversation. It seems unlikely that all of these have the same role in a child's psychological development and one of the main tasks of later chapters will be to identify the separate consequences of different types of 'maternal deprivation'. It is also evident that many of the qualities required for good mothering also apply to other relationships experienced by the child. It is perhaps preferable to concentrate on the various requirements for normal development rather than to attempt any rather artificial separation of functions which are specifically those of the mother.

3 Short-Term Effects of 'Maternal Deprivation'

There can be no clear-cut demarcation between short-term and long-term effects of 'maternal deprivation', as they blend into one another. Nevertheless, it is useful for the purposes of discussion to consider consequences in this way. The effects will be considered 'short-term' when they refer to the immediate response to a depriving experience and to the behaviour shown over the next few months. 'Long-term' will be primarily used to refer to the effects seen some years later, either following a brief period of deprivation or after continuous and prolonged privation. Intermediate effects will not be considered separately but will be mentioned in either context when they throw light on the psychological mechanisms involved.

Before turning to a discussion of possible variables and mechanisms it is necessary to consider what short-term effects have been attributed to 'deprivation'. As the literature has been previously well reviewed from several different viewpoints and as, for the most part, the observations (as distinct from the interpretations) are not in dispute, this introduction will be quite brief.

Short-term effects have been most studied with respect to children admitted to hospital or to a residential nursery (Vernon, Foley, Sipowicz and Schuman, 1965; Yarrow, 1964). There is good evidence that many (but not all) young children show an immediate reaction of acute distress and crying (what has been called the period of 'protest'), followed by misery and apathy (the phase of 'despair'), and finally there may be a stage when the child becomes apparently contented and seems to lose interest in his parents ('detachment' in Robertson's and Bowlby's terms) (Bowlby, 1958a, 1962, 1968; Robertson and Bowlby, 1952). That these reactions occur is well established.

What remains controversial is their clinical significance and the psychological mechanisms involved.

The other syndrome seen as an early response to 'maternal deprivation' is developmental retardation (Provence and Lipton, 1962). There may be a global impairment of developmental progress but language and social responsiveness are usually most affected.

The psychological processes involved in these reactions will be considered by first examining the factors which modify the reactions and then discussing the possible mechanisms involved.

Modifying factors
Age of child

Systematic observations of children admitted to hospital have shown that emotional distress is most marked in children aged six months to four years, but even in this age group it occurs in only some children (Illingworth and Holt, 1955; Prugh, Staub, Sands, Kirschbaum and Lenihan, 1953; Schaffer and Callender, 1959). Distress does occur in some older children admitted to hospital but it tends to be less severe, less prolonged and it occurs in a lower proportion of children. Under the age of about six months there is usually *no* distress associated with admission to hospital.

The effect of age on developmental retardation associated with institutional care is quite different, suggesting that different psychological mechanisms are involved. Infants under the age of six months in hospitals, or other institutions where there is little stimulation, vocalize little and become socially unresponsive (Brodbeck and Irwin, 1946; Provence and Lipton, 1962; Schaffer and Callender, 1959). Deviations in language, social and motor development have been reported as early as the second month. However, there is no particular upper age restriction on this reaction which also occurs in older children.

Sex of child

The findings on sex differences are somewhat contradictory and no differences have been found in many studies (Vernon *et al.*, 1965), but where there has been a sex difference, both in young subhuman primates and in children, the male has usually been found to be the more vulnerable to the adverse effects of separation experiences (Sackett, 1968; Spencer-Booth and Hinde, 1971a; Stacey *et al.*, 1970). If this tentative finding is confirmed it would be in keeping with the evidence suggesting that young males may be generally more susceptible than females to psychological stress, as certainly they are to biological stress (Rutter, 1970).

Temperament of child

There is ample evidence that individuals differ strikingly in their behaviour and responsiveness from early infancy (Berger and Passingham, 1972). A variety of studies have shown that infants differ in their psychophysiological characteristics (Steinschneider, 1967), response to stimulation (Bridger and Birns, 1968), oral activity (Korner, Chuck and Dontchos, 1968), behavioural style and response to new situations (Thomas, Chess and Birch, 1968; Thomas, Chess, Birch, Hertzig and Korn, 1963). The determinants of these individual differences are not fully understood, but sex-linked factors (Berger and Passingham, 1972), genetic mechanisms (Freed-man and Keller, 1963), perinatal trauma (Ucko, 1965) and environmental influences (Zigler, 1966) probably all play a part. The importance of these individual differences has been shown by their association with the child's later behavioural disturbance (Rutter, Birch, Thomas and Chess, 1964; Thomas, Chess and Birch, 1968) and educational performance (Kagan, 1965).

Until very recently, however, there has been little investigation of temperamental differences in relation to children's responses to hospital admission or other forms of separation. The studies already mentioned suggest the importance of temperamental attributes and one of the most striking features of all investigations of 'deprivation' has been the enormous variation in the way individuals have reacted. A pilot study by Stacey and her colleagues (1970) has now shown that part of this individual variation can be accounted for in terms of what the children were like prior to the separation experience. Those who were said to make poor relationships with adults and other children, and to be socially inhibited, uncommunicative and aggressive, were the ones most likely to be disturbed by admission to hospital. Temperamental differences have also been found to be important with respect to the developmental retardation shown by infants in a depriving environment. In a study of infants under six months of age, the most active infants were the ones who showed the least drop in developmental quotient (Schaffer, 1966).

Previous mother–child relationship

The fact that distress following separation does not usually occur in infants under the age of six months has already been mentioned. As this is about the age that maternal attachment becomes firm (Schaffer and Emerson, 1964), it may be accepted as circumstantial evidence that the child probably needs to have developed a relationship before he can show emotional distress with a separation experience. Apart from this well-established finding, the human evidence on the importance, or otherwise, of the child's previous relationship with his mother is extremely weak. On the whole it appears that short-term distress is less if the child had a good relationship before separation (Vernon et al., 1965). It has also been suggested that disturbance is less likely to occur where the child has had more caretakers and therefore less intense and less exclusive attachments (Mead, 1962), but the evidence for this is anecdotal.

The most impressive evidence on the importance of mother–child relationships in response to separation comes from animal work: a series of very important investigations by Hinde and his colleagues has thrown much-needed new light on the question. In a longitudinal study of the effects of a short period of separation on young rhesus monkeys, they found that the infants who showed the greatest disturbance following separation were those who had shown the most 'tension' in their relationship with their mother prior to separation (Hinde and Spencer-Booth, 1970). 'Tension' was operationally defined in terms of the frequency of maternal rejections and the role of the infant in maintaining proximity to his mother. While results from animal work cannot be directly applied to humans, these findings strongly suggest that the area requires further exploration in children.

The differences in separation response between different species of monkey are also relevant in this context (Kaufman and Rosenblum, 1969a, 1969b). Pigtail macaques have been found to exhibit greater distress on separation than do bonnet macaques and it has been suggested that this is explicable in terms of differences in the mother–infant relationship between the two species. Bonnet macaques are normally less dependent on their mothers than are pigtails; they spend more time in social play, more often approach other members of the group and leave their mothers for longer periods, going longer distances. In the same way, bonnet mothers are more permissive than pigtail mothers. As a result of this, during the period of separation the bonnet infants are more likely to achieve an association with another adult who thereby produces substitute mothering. In contrast pigtails become withdrawn and isolated following the first acute distress and do not attach to other adults. This difference seems to be due to the previous interactional experiences in the two species rather than to any general differences in maternal solicitude.

Previous separation experiences

It is generally supposed that children who have experienced separation once become sensitized so that later similar experiences are likely to be especially traumatic for them (Ainsworth, 1962), but there is remarkably little evidence on this point. Spencer-Booth and Hinde (1971a) found that infant rhesus monkeys separated for the second time responded in much the same way as those separated for the first time at the same age. In humans, too, there is surprisingly little to support the notion of a sensitizing effect. What little evidence there is suggests that whether this happens depends greatly on the nature of the first separation. Where children have had a previously unhappy experience of separation there is some suggestion that they are more likely to respond adversely to hospital admission than are children without such a previous stress (Vernon *et al.*, 1965). On the other hand, it appears that if the separations have been happy ones, there may be the reverse effect. Thus Stacey *et al.* (1970) found that children who were undisturbed by hospital admission were more likely than the distressed children to have had *more* 'normal' separation experiences such as staying overnight with friends or relatives, having baby-sitters, attending nursery school and being left all day with a familiar person. There is too little evidence to be dogmatic on the matter and further research on the issue should be rewarding, but it seems that a child's response to a separation experience may be influenced for the better or worse by the nature of previous separations.

Duration of separation/deprivation

Even with short-term responses to separation/deprivation it seems that distress may be greater the longer that the experience lasts, although not much is known on this point. Heinicke and Westheimer (1965) in a study of ten children placed in a residential nursery, found more disturbance at the end of the separation period in the four children separated for seven to twenty-one weeks than in the six children separated for less than three weeks. Similarly in a study of rhesus monkeys, Hinde and Spencer-Booth (1971b) found that distress was greater following a thirteen-day separation than that after a six-day separation.

Different effect of separation and strange environment

Douglas and Blomfield (1958) found that long-term ill-effects generally followed separation *only* when separation was accompanied by change of environment. This finding, and the fact that most studies of the short-term effects of separation concern children in strange environments such as a hospital, has led to the suggestion that the distress may be due to the environment rather than the separation as such. To examine this question it is necessary to determine what happens when a child is present in a strange setting *with* his mother and conversely what happens if he is left at home without his mother. Rheingold (1969) has examined the first question with respect to the immediate responses of ten-month-old infants. She found very little distress when infants were placed in a strange environment *with* their mother, but considerable distress when placed there on their own or with a stranger. Similar results were reported by Ainsworth and Wittig (1969) in a study of twelve-month-old infants. Many (but not all) infants showed some distress when their mothers left them in a room which they had entered together a few moments previously. Morgan and Ricciuti (1969) found that over a third of ten- to twelve-month-old infants reacted negatively to strangers even when sitting on their mother's lap but that a negative reaction was much more likely if the infant was across the room from his mother. Negative reactions also occurred more often when the stranger touched the baby than when he made a 'peek-a-boo'-like head movement without approaching. It may be concluded that strange persons and strange environments are fear-provoking stimuli for infants, but that the presence of the mother goes a long way to reducing or eliminating the distress in a novel setting.

These findings all apply to distress during separations of a few minutes. Less is known about longer separations but the findings seem to be similar. Children's disturbance during hospital admission is greatly reduced if they are admitted together with their mother or if there is daily visiting by parents (Faust, Jackson, Cermak, Burtt and Winkley, 1952; Illingworth and Holt, 1955; Prugh *et al.*, 1953). Unfortunately, it is not possible from these studies to determine how much reduction in distress was due to the mother's presence and how much to other factors, as the experimental programmes included many features such as special play facilities, careful preparation of the children for admission and the reduction of potentially traumatic procedures such, as venipunctures and enemas.

There are several descriptions suggesting that the presence of the child's mother is the crucial variable (MacCarthy, Lindsay and Morris, 1962; Mićić, 1962; Robertson, 1958, 1962) but only two studies which have isolated this factor in a systematic fashion. Fagin (1966), in a comparison of two groups of thirty children, one admitted to hospital alone and one with their mothers, found distress almost entirely eliminated when the mothers were there. In contrast, Vernon, Foley and Schulman (1967) found only a small (but significant) difference due to the mother's presence, suggesting that other factors designed to reduce the stress of hospital admission were of considerable importance.

Bowlby (1969) has pointed out that the anecdotal evidence on how young children behave during family holidays also suggests that infants in a strange environment *with* their parents usually show little distress. Although a few young children may be upset in such conditions, prolonged or marked disturbance is quite uncommon.

There is also extensive evidence from animal studies that mothers, or even mother-surrogates (such as a cloth figure), have a marked effect in imparting security to infants placed in a strange or frightening situation. This has been well shown for rhesus monkeys by Harlow and his colleagues (e.g. Harlow and Harlow, 1965) and has been noted in goats by Liddell (1950).

On the second question – how infants react when left by their mothers while remaining in a familiar situation – there are anecdotal reports of the occurrence of distress following loss of the mother-figure occurring in infants who remained in their home environment (Deutsch, 1919; Spiro, 1958). On the other hand, the Robertsons (see page 44) have found that distress need not occur in this situation. Systematic studies are needed but pose difficulties in that, at least for longer separations, the children would have to be left with someone and if the setting were to be familiar the person would likely be known to the child. As discussed below, the presence of a familiar person has similar stress-reducing properties to the mother's presence.

However, the question has been studied in subhuman primates reared in a group setting (Kaufman and Rosenblum, 1969a, 1969b; Spencer-Booth and Hindle, 1971a, 1971b). It is clear from these studies that infant monkeys show acute distress when their mothers are taken away, the infants remaining in their usual environment.

The extent to which the sequence of protest, despair and detachment is separation-specific is a matter of some interest. It seems that the protest state of acute distress and clinging is non-specific. Mason (1967) has found similar effects in chimpanzees following restraint, noise and stimulant drugs. Evidence is lacking but the stages of despair and detachment *might* be more specific to separation experiences.

In summary, both separation and a strange environment occurring individually may produce distress in infants, but distress is most marked when both occur together. The effects of a strange environment are less consistent and it seems that it is the nature of the strangeness as well as the presence of a novel stimulus which is important. Indeed, some novel stimuli may be pleasurable to the child. Nevertheless, on the whole, it appears that separations may be less stressful if the infant remains in a familiar environment. Conversely, strange environments are much less stressful if the infant is present with his mother. The fact that this effect is more marked and more consistent than the ameleriorating effect of a familiar environment during separations suggests that separation may be of more basic importance. However, it is not possible to compare meaningfully separation and strangeness without further specification. Clearly, the relative importance of each will vary with the environmental circumstances.

Presence of persons other than the mother

One of the problems in comparing the effects of separation and a strange environment has been the confounding effect of the presence of other persons. Several studies have shown that familiar people, other than the mother, also reduce children's distress in strange situations. In 1943, Arsenian demonstrated that children from a residential nursery showed distress when introduced to a strange situation but that this was often less when they were accompanied by one of the nursery helpers with whom they were familiar. With 'dependent' children the presence of a substitute mother was not as effective as that of the true mother. In young adults, too, the presence of a friend (but not a stranger) reduced autonomic disturbance in a stress situation (Kissel, 1965).

In their study of children admitted to a residential nursery, Heinicke and Westheimer (1965) found that distress was much reduced in those children admitted with a sib. This was so in spite of the fact that the sibs were too young to take on a caretaking role.

Animal work leads to similar conclusions. The short-term effects of infant–infant separation in rhesus monkeys reared apart from their mothers seem similar to the effects of mother–infant separation (Suomi, Harlow and Domek, 1970). Also, the presence of another monkey of the same age tends to reduce the emotional disturbance of young rhesus monkeys in a strange situation (Mason, 1960).

As already noted, children form attachments with many people other than their mother and it is evident that the presence of familiar persons acts to reduce stress in a strange situation just as the presence of the mother does. It is important to note in this connection that bonds form with people who have no caretaking role towards the child and the presence of a peer or sib reduces stress in similar fashion to the presence of a parent-surrogate. On the whole children are less distressed with their mother than with some other person so that it would be wrong to conclude that any individual does equally well. But there is no evidence that it is being a mother that is important. On the basis of the very scanty available evidence it seems more likely that the stress-reducing properties of the accompanying person are related to the strength of bond formation. It may be hypothesized that where the bond is strongest with the mother she will have the greatest stress-reducing properties, where bonds are stronger with someone else she will not.

Nature of circumstances during separation/deprivation

The beneficial effect of improved hospital conditions in reducing children's distress following admission has already been mentioned (Faust *et al.*, 1952; Prugh *et al.*, 1953). Emotional disturbance is far from universal in children admitted to hospital (Davenport and Werry, 1970). It is quite evident that the circumstances experienced by an infant during separation or institutional care make a major difference to the infant's emotional response, but which environmental factors are the most important in this connection are largely unknown. Since Burlingham and Freud's (1942, 1944) important early studies at the Hampstead Nursery, much emphasis has been placed on the provision of high-quality substitute maternal care involving stability, affection and active involvement. In hospital, careful attention has also been paid to the reduction of unpleasant procedures and the adequate preparation of the child for those which are unavoidable.

The provision of ample toys with play facilities supervised by trained workers has been advocated by paediatricians (Jolly, 1969) on the grounds that boredom leads to distress. A recent experimental investigation of ten-month-old infants by Rheingold and Samuels (1969) has now provided support for this view. Not surprisingly, children with their mothers but without toys fussed and fretted more than children who had both their mothers present and toys to play with. Nevertheless, it should be noted that this study did not show whether or not toys will reduce distress in children *without* their mothers.

The importance of environmental stimulation in counteracting developmental retardation has been shown in several studies. Rheingold (1956) showed that institutional infants became more socially responsive when provided with extra individual attention and communication. In a later study she showed that the vocalizations of three-month-old infants can be increased by smiling, speaking to them and touching them (Rheingold, Gewirtz, and Ross, 1959). Casler (1965) found that daily tactile stimulation diminished the degree of retardation in institutional children. White (1967, 1971) has shown that the onset of hand regard, visually directed reaching and the growth of visual attentiveness in human infants are significantly improved by providing extra handling, placing the infant so he can look around better, putting bright striped mittens on his hands to attract his attention, and by making sure that there are plenty of mobiles and other interesting things for him to watch. The difficulty of determining exactly which experience had which effect is illustrated by Korner and Grobstein's (1966) finding that picking up tearful infants not only soothed them but also led to increased visual alertness and scanning of the environment.

Sayegh and Dennis (1965) showed a gain in developmental quotient as a result of giving institutional infants an hour's extra attention per day. Schaffer has shown similar effects. He found that eleven- to fourteen-week-old infants in a baby home with a high degree of measured social stimulation showed no developmental retardation, whereas those in a hospital with a low degree of stimulation were retarded (Schaffer, 1965). In both cases the children were admitted for only short periods and following discharge the developmental quotients in the two groups were comparable. This showed that the retardation was a function of the institution and not the type of children admitted. A further study of twenty-four-week-old infants showed that the developmental quotient could be immediately raised following a period of stimulation, suggesting that the retardation was a function of the environmental situation rather than a measure of reduced organismic capacity (Schaffer and Emerson, 1968). Of course, if non-stimulating conditions were to continue for long enough a true reduction in capacity might occur, but the experiment was solely concerned with short-term effects.

Possible mechanisms

As evident from the findings already discussed, the factors modifying the two main short-term effects of deprivation (distress and retardation) are rather different. This suggests that different psychological mechanisms may be involved and possible explanations will have to be considered separately for each.

Separation or a strange environment?

This question has already been discussed in connection with modifying factors. Physical illness or unpleasant medical (and surgical) procedures may be stressful experiences to young children, but the fact that the adverse effects of admission to a residential nursery are so similar to those following admission to hospital argues against this being the main factor in the distress associated with separation. Experimental studies on the beneficial effect of toys and on the results of measures designed to make hospital admission less traumatic certainly suggest that environmental factors other than separation may sometimes play an important part in the production of the acute distress associated with hospital admission. The finding that distress is much less common in some hospitals than in others supports the same conclusion.

Nevertheless, the evidence already discussed suggests that separation from family members is probably a more basic cause of emotional distress. When with parents, young children may even find a strange environment interesting and altogether a positive experience. However, much depends on what sort of strange environment it is and some can be quite frightening to young children.

The finding that the developmental retardation of children in hospital can be reversed without altering the strangeness of the environment suggests that strangeness is not an important factor in causing retardation.

Separation or disturbed mother–infant relationship?

The analyses of just what it is in a separation experience which makes it have adverse effects (or conversely which prevents it having such effects) provides many methodological problems, not the least of which is the great difficulty of isolating each of the elements. This is most readily done in an experimental design and ethical considerations mean that we have to turn to animal studies for an answer.

This question has been investigated by Hinde and his co-workers in a carefully controlled set of studies of rhesus monkeys (Hinde, 1972; Hinde and Spencer-Booth, 1970). There are three main findings which are relevant in this connection. Firstly, as noted above, infants' distress following separation is a function of both the pre-separation and the contemporaneous mother–infant relationship. Secondly, changes in mother–infant interaction from day to day after reunion largely depend on the mother. Thirdly, infants showed much *less* post-separation distress and more *normal* mother–infant interaction when they themselves were removed to a strange place for thirteen days and then restored to their mother than when the mothers were removed to a strange place for a similar period. In other words the monkey equivalent of 'mother goes to hospital' led to *more* disturbance than did the monkey equivalent of 'baby goes to hospital'. These are important and striking findings, particularly as the third observation runs counter to what one might expect. Hinde has argued convincingly that the probable explanation is that the infants' post-separation distress is not primarily due to the separation as such but rather to the consequent disturbance in maternal behaviour. Where separation leads to distortions in the mother's interaction with the infant, the infant suffers. Where separation does *not* affect the mother's behaviour, the distress in the infant is very much less.

As Hinde has been most careful to point out, it is necessary to be cautious in generalizing the finding to other species and it is important to draw parallels at the right level. For example, it may well be that in humans the infant's role in determining mother–infant interaction is greater than in the rhesus monkey. Nevertheless, it seems reasonable to suggest that if a disturbed mother–infant interaction is the mediating factor in separation distress in rhesus monkeys then it may also be so in humans, as the reactions to separation appear so similar in other respects in the two species. Hinde's hypothesis is most important in both its theoretical and practical implications; human research into the question is urgently called for. Some of the Robertsons' work is relevant here, but as it refers more directly to the effects of deprivation of maternal care it will be discussed in the next section.

Separation or deprivation of maternal care?

Most human studies of distress following separation have been concerned with children admitted to hospital or to a residential nursery, confounding the effects of separation and of deprivation of maternal care. In this context, 'separation' is used to refer to the physical loss of the mother-figure but not necessarily of mothering. 'Deprivation' refers to the loss of maternal care but not necessarily of the mother-figure (Howells, 1970). There is ample evidence that even in good institutions the maternal care provided differs in both quantity and quality from that experienced in a family setting (David and Appell, 1961; King, Raynes and Tizard, 1971; Rheingold, 1960; Tizard and Tizard, 1971).

The question, then, is whether separation from a *person* to whom bonds of attachment have developed (in this case the mother) can lead to distress even though there is a normal provision of good maternal care and no other environmental stress. Bowlby (1961, 1968, 1969; Bowlby and Parkes, 1970) has argued over many years that it can. In short, he suggests that separation constitutes a *grief* reaction or a response to bereavement. It is the loss of a *person* which is crucial, not just the loss of maternal care (although he has always emphasized that the damage is much greater when both occur together). This is an important question, the answer to which has far-reaching implications concerning the avoidance of distress during separation experiences.

There cannot be much animal evidence on this point in that separation from mother in most animal species almost inevitably leads to some deprivation of maternal care. In humans, however, this need not be the case. The mother may be absent but yet perfectly adequate care be provided by other people. It will not, of course, be quite the *same* as that given by the mother in that the personal style of interaction will differ, but it may easily be of similar quality and quantity.

Perhaps the most convincing evidence that separation is a key variable is the finding that the presence of sibs or other familiar persons greatly ameliorates children's distress following admission or in some other stress situation. Distress seems to be less even though the accompanying person neither provides nor improves maternal care.

Investigations of children separated from familiar persons but remaining in a small family group would help clarify the situation. In this connection, the Robertsons' valuable films of children in brief separation are most informative (Robertson and Robertson, 1967, 1968a, 1968b). The film showing the response of a two year old's admission to hospital (Robertson, 1952) and the short stay of a seventeen-month-old boy in a residential nursery (Robertson and Robertson, 1968b) clearly illustrated the acute distress which often occurs when children are separated *and* in a strange and potentially stressful situation. They have also made two films of what happens when children of a similar age are separated from their parents but remain in a small family setting (the Robertsons' home). Both the children they studied showed signs of mild stress or insecurity, but basically they maintained developmental progress and adapted to the change. While there was evidence of the tension implicit in the separation experience, their reactions were vastly different to the marked psychological disturbance shown by the children admitted to hospital or to a residential nursery. With the fact of separation held constant, distress could be very greatly ameliorated by improving maternal care *during* the separation. Although the Robertsons' study design was quite different to that used with rhesus monkeys by Hinde it should be noted that the conclusions are similar; namely that it is not separation as such which is the key factor but rather the accompanying distortion of the mother–child relationship. Controlled comparisons of larger numbers of children are obviously needed but the available findings suggest that although separation from mother may induce some stress, the disturbance which follows this alone is very much less than that which occurs when separation is accompanied by deprivation of maternal care.

However, before concluding that it is the deprivation of maternal care which leads to the distress, it is necessary to emphasize again that separation and bond disruption cannot be equated. Was there anything in the Robertsons' foster-home situation which was *not* present in the residential nursery or hospital and which may have enabled the children to maintain bonds during separation? In this connection, one difference stands out. Whereas none of the adults in the nursery was known to John (the seventeen month old admitted for nine days to a residential nursery), Kate and Jane, the two children fostered by the Robertsons, had both met them *before* the separation. The presence of a familiar adult may have helped the children maintain bonds. If this is so, only brief acquaintance may be sufficient for the adult to be regarded as 'familiar'. The children had only been introduced to the Robertsons for the first time in the few weeks prior to separation.

There was one other difference relevant to the maintenance of bonds. The Robertsons took special care to talk to the children about their mothers and so keep alive memories during the separation. For the same reasons they endeavoured to follow the children's known daily routines and to keep to the overall pattern of discipline and child-rearing to which they were accustomed. This was not possible to the same extent in the residential nursery where the staff knew little about the children and their patterns of family life.

In short, the findings are entirely compatible with a hypothesis that bond disruption is the key variable, so long as it is recognized that this is not a necessary consequence of separation. The extensive evidence already discussed, of the marked comforting effect of a familiar figure during a stress situation (even though maternal care is not altered), also provides support for this view and argues against deprivation of maternal care being accepted as a sufficient explanation.

On the other hand, there were differences between the care provided by the Robertsons and that given in hospital or the residential nursery. As no systematic measures of care were recorded, it is only possible to speculate on the differences using what is known about hospital and nursery care and what is shown in the Robertsons' films. The nursery in which John showed such severe distress was well staffed with trained people and there was ample provision of toys. While a general reduction in perceptual stimulation or in the range of daily life experiences may well play an important part in the genesis of distress in *other* situations, it is very unlikely that this was the case with John. If this is so, it means that there must be some other crucial ingredient in maternal care which is needed to prevent the distress seen in many children admitted to hospital or to a residential nursery.

It is likely that this ingredient is the opportunity for a continuing intense personal interaction with the same individual or individuals over time. This did not occur in the nursery where care was on a work-assignment basis, with nurses turning to whatever task came to hand with whichever children were concerned. This, together with the organization of off-duty times, meant that John had to interact with a varying group of adults, none of whom was specifically allocated to look after him, and in a situation where it was unpredictable (to him) who would be available to deal with him at different times. In contrast, in the Robertsons' home the children had only two adults looking after them and one of these was always present and available to provide care, comfort or play as was required. This is a situation which allows attachments to develop and in fact the children *did* develop attachments to the Robertsons during their brief spell with them. This did not occur with John in the residential nursery. If this emphasis is correct, then the necessary ingredient in maternal care (to prevent distress during separation) is a personal and continuing interaction with the child which can provide a basis for bond formation.

The available evidence does not allow a choice between the two explanations for the distress so often seen during separation experiences – namely bond disruption and impairment of attachment behaviour (in general rather than to the person who is absent). However, in both cases it appears that separation *per se* is not the key factor, but that some distortion or disruption of the bonding process is crucial. From the rather slender circumstantial evidence which is available it would seem likely that both factors probably play an important part in the genesis of distress. Which factor makes the most difference is not known (in any case this is likely to vary with individual circumstances). Indeed, further study is required to determine whether the two hypothesized factors are actually the relevant ones. Whereas the evidence seems to point to their influence, the relevant data are weak.

The explanation for developmental retardation must be quite different, because severe retardation has been found in children born in, or admitted to, institutions in the first month of life at a time when they have yet to develop any attachments and have a very limited ability to differentiate between the adults providing care (Dennis, 1960), and the retardation is reversible simply by increasing stimulation without altering the separation situation. Also, again separation as such cannot be the explanation because some studies of institutional children have failed to find any retardation in spite of the fact that all have experienced separation from parents.

The findings are reasonably clear-cut that some form of privation of stimulation rather than any type of separation is responsible for the retardation. What remains uncertain is the relative importance for each type of developmental retardation (the retardation may affect a variety of different developmental functions, such as speech, motor coordination and bladder control) of different types of stimulation – social, perceptual, motor, experiential and linguistic. It is highly likely that different developmental functions require different forms of stimulation for their development, but the point has been little investigated.

Deprivation or privation?

The above evidence also makes it clear that the retardation is due to a *lack* of stimulation and not to the *loss* of stimulation. Accordingly, privation is a more correct description than deprivation.

Again the situation is different for the syndrome of distress. Children who have never developed attachments seem *not* to show this syndrome of distress (although they have other disturbances – see chapters 4 and 5 on long-term consequences of deprivation). Accordingly, the distress syndrome is probably due to 'deprivation', not to privation. Whether the 'deprivation' involves disruption of a bond or the loss of attachment opportunities is considered below. Very little is known about the emotional consequences of loss other than in the context of separation from a familiar person.

Separation from mother or separation from a familiar person?

The evidence that distress is much reduced by the presence of a brother or sister or a friend even when the mother remains absent strongly suggests that there is nothing specific about mother separation. Indeed it is most curious that studies of children in hospital or a residential nursery are nearly always considered as examples of separation from mother when in fact they consist of separation from mother *and* father *and* sibs *and* the home environment. There are no studies of the short-term effects of paternal absence and the influence of the father has been greatly neglected. The author's unsystematic observations of young children in families where the father spends occasional periods away from home suggest that in many families this is as likely to lead to emotional distress as is the absence of the mother. Whether or not this is so, and if it is *why*, requires investigation.

Amelioration of distress during maternal absence does not occur if the person with the child is unfamiliar, and the degree of amelioration varies greatly according to which family member or friend is present. This is not a function of a mothering role because distress is reduced even with younger sibs of two or three years. The available evidence suggests that the relevant variable is the strength of the child's attachment to the person. The most parsimonious explanation of the research findings suggests that a child needs to have the presence of a person to whom he is attached but it is irrelevant whether or not this person is his mother. He also needs to have adequate maternal care and if this is not provided he suffers. But it appears that this need not be given by the person to whom he is most attached. If this hypothesis is correct (and it requires rigorous testing) then the emphasis on attachment behaviour and bonding by Bowlby (1968, 1969) and others is correct, but its linking with maternal care is misleading. The implications for practical policy are also different from an exclusive maternal attachment view. If it is bond formation which is important (rather than mother–child bond formation), it is in a child's interest to encourage attachment to several people, not just one, so that if one person is away another is present. Furthermore, from this point of view separation should not be regarded as synonymous with bond disruption. If a child is used to short stays with friends and relatives in happy circumstances he is more likely to learn that separations are temporary and can be pleasant. Accordingly, later unavoidable separations of an unhappy kind (such as hospitalization of parent or child) are likely to be less traumatic.

So far as can be determined. developmental retardation is not due to bond disruption of any type but rather to privation of some type of care or stimulation.

Disruption of all bonds or disruption of one of several bonds?

The argument above rather depends on the assumption that disruption of one bond is less traumatic if other bonds exist than if that is the only bond. It might seem obvious that this should be the case but evidence in support is largely lacking. Rosenblum (1971a) has some preliminary evidence that distress following mother–infant separation in squirrel monkeys is less when other adult monkeys ('aunts') have also mothered the infant and remain available during the separation. The Robertsons' film on Jane, the seventeen-month-old child they fostered for ten days, showed that there was some mild tension associated with the child's separation from the Robertsons at the time of the mother's return home (Robertson and Robertson, 1968a). This and other observations in the literature suggest that there can be *some* stress associated with even the disruption of one of many bonds. However, the same observations suggest that the stress is very much less than in the case of the disruption of a solitary bond. The matter needs systematic study.

Disruption of bonds or loss of bonding behaviour?

It has already been noted that the distress associated with admission to a strange residential nursery involves *both* separation from all familiar people *and* care which lacks intensity and individuality so that the attachments the child is accustomed to cannot redevelop. Which is more important? Again evidence is largely lacking, although once more the Robertsons' films provide a lead. The children they fostered had known them only a few weeks before the separation experience so that prior bonds with the children were probably quite weak. But they were familiar to the children and the children's fathers continued to visit, so the break was only partial.

On the extremely slender anecdotal evidence available it might be hypothesized that either separation from all familiar people *or* care which did not allow attachments are likely to be stressful to a young child, and that both are influential. The issue requires investigation. It should be noted in passing that substitute care for children separated from their families frequently involves deprivation of both.

Discussion

The evidence strongly points to the operation of quite different psychological mechanisms in the genesis of acute distress and of developmental retardation as short-term responses to 'deprivation'. The retardation appears explicable in terms of a privation or lack (rather than loss) of environmental 'stimulation'. It remains uncertain whether social stimulation as provided by interaction with people, perceptual and motor stimulation as provided by play, experiences and activities, or linguistic stimulation as provided by conversation and meaningful talk on an individual basis is most important. Probably all three are needed but for rather different aspects of development.

In contrast the syndrome of distress (as shown by the sequence of protest, despair and detachment) is probably due to deprivation (i.e. loss rather than lack) of some aspect of bonding or attachment behaviour. Whether the loss of a particular person to whom the child is attached or rather the general loss of any opportunity to develop attachments is the more important remains uncertain. Whereas these consequences may occur, and perhaps particularly occur, with separation from the mother, it should be noted that there is nothing to suggest that her role is a specific one in this connection, and a good deal of evidence to suggest that it is not. The mother is usually the person who has done most for the child, is most familiar to the child and has given most comfort. For all these reasons her presence is likely to be more important than anyone else's. But her importance stems from her contact with the child, and her relative importance compared with other family members will depend on the constellation of relationships in each particular family. In the writer's view, theories of mothering have frequently been too mechanical in equating separation with bond disruption, too restricted in regarding the mother as the only person important in a child's life, and too narrow in considering love as the only important element in maternal care.

This review has been concerned with the psychological mechanisms involved in the short-term effects of deprivation on the child. However, it is vital not to overlook the important evidence (briefly noted above) that children vary greatly in their response to separation and deprivation. Parent–child interaction is an active ongoing two-way process with the child's own attributes being an important determinant of how the interaction develops (Bell, 1968). Study of this rather neglected side of the dyad is likely to prove rewarding.

Conclusions

Evidence on the factors modifying or influencing children's responses to short-term separation or deprivation has been reviewed and possible psychological mechanisms have been considered. It is concluded that the syndrome of distress (protest, despair, detachment) is probably due to a disruption or distortion of the bonding process (not necessarily with the mother), and that the syndrome of developmental retardation is probably due to a privation of social, perceptual and linguistic stimulation.

4 Long-Term Consequences: Modifying Factors

The initial case for regarding 'maternal deprivation' as the cause of long-term disturbance rests largely on clinical studies. Bender (1947), Bowlby (1946) and others (reviewed in Bowlby, 1951) noted the frequency with which both delinquency and affectionless psychopathy were associated with multiple separation experiences and institutional care. A variety of investigations have found an association between delinquency and broken homes (see reviews by Wootton, 1959, and Yarrow 1961). Studies of children reared in institutions have also shown a high level of language retardation and mental subnormality (Goldfarb, 1945a, 1945b; Pringle and Tanner, 1958; Provence and Lipton, 1962). Children already handicapped by organic brain impairment such as in Down's syndrome ('mongolism') make less progress in institutions than they do at home (Francis, 1971; Lyle, 1959, 1960; Stedman and Eichorn, 1964). Following on early paediatric observations that institutional children often fail to gain weight properly (Bakwin, 1949), more recent investigations have shown a connection between dwarfism and growth failure on the one hand and a history of maternal rejection and lack of warmth on the other (Patton and Gardner, 1963). The evidence linking maternal deprivation with depression mostly concerns adult patients (Rutter, 1971a) but family disruption has also been found in association with depression in children (Caplan and Douglas, 1969).

It may be concluded that disorders of conduct, personality, language, cognition and physical growth have all been found to occur in children with serious disturbances in their early family life, which have been included under the rather loose general heading of 'maternal deprivation'. However, the early family disturbances reported, as well as the later outcomes, are rather heterogeneous and, as with short-term effects, it remains to be determined which type of 'deprivation' has which long-term consequence.

Long-term effects of early life experiences

As it is sometimes claimed that psychological development is genetically determined to an extent which leaves little room for environmental influences to have any significant effects, it may be useful to consider some of the evidence that early life experiences can have a major impact on later functioning.

The most convincing evidence comes from experimental animal work where it is possible to control the relevant variables in a fashion that allows the effects of each to be measured. There are numerous studies which show quite clearly that environmental manipulations can have a very fundamental and long-lasting effect on development. They also demonstrate that experimental manipulations of one sort of behaviour may influence the development of an apparently different sort of behaviour.

The animal evidence in support of these statements is so extensive (Hinde, 1970; Sluckin, 1970; Thompson and Grusec, 1970) that only a small number of examples can be included to illustrate the wide range of such effects on development of early life experiences and to note the wide range of species in which the effects have been shown. Perhaps the best known example of early learning with a persisting influence into adult life is the phenomenon of 'imprinting' (Hinde, 1970). During a short sensitive period in early infancy nidifugous birds will follow a wide range of moving objects. The objects they learn to follow during this sensitive phase are the ones to which attachments develop and the birds will continue to exhibit following behaviour to matchboxes, men or whatever other objects upon which they become imprinted. Conversely they will *not* follow objects upon which they have *not* been imprinted – thus they will not follow their own mother if she was not present during the 'imprinting' phase. A similar phenomenon (but less consistent and arising slightly later) influences adult choice of sexual object (Fabricius, 1962). Birds which learn to follow humans in early life will on reaching maturity often also exhibit sexual behaviour towards humans. The effects of early experience on the stimuli eliciting later social or reproductive behaviour have also been shown in fish, mice, lambs, guinea pigs, indeed in almost all vertebrate groups (Hinde, 1970).

A wide range of studies (e.g. Bronfenbrenner, 1968; McCandless, 1964) have shown the cognitive and perceptual deficiencies which follow early stimulus deprivation. For example, it has been found that patterned visual stimulation is important in the development of visually guided behaviour (Riesen, 1965). Held and his colleagues (Hein and Held, 1967; Held and Bauer, 1967; Held and Hein, 1963) have gone further and demonstrated with both cats and monkeys that *active*, as distinct from passive, visual experience was necessary. Animals whose visual experience was the result of their own active movements showed superior judgement of distance and space (as judged by paw placing and the visual cliff experiment) to those whose visual experience was the result of their being passively transported. A simple apparatus which allowed only progressive movement around a circular box controlled the amount of visual experience in the two cases.

Levine (1962) and others have shown the far-reaching psychological and physical effects (in rats) of quite minor stimulation in early infancy. Stimulated rats showed early eye opening, less 'emotionality', greater weight gain and early maturation of certain glandular functions associated with response to stress. There are some inter-species differences in the effects of stimulation and the mechanisms are ill-understood. Some of the changes evidently result from the direct action on the young, but some seem to be due to changes in the behaviour of the mother toward her offspring (Barnett and Burn, 1967).

The sometimes long-term effects of brief periods of separation in infancy in rhesus monkeys has been observed by Hinde and Spencer-Booth (1971b; Spencer-Booth and Hinde, 1971b). Five months after the separation experience, although their behaviour lay within normal limits, the separated infants approached and interacted with strange objects in a strange situation less readily than did the controls. Some of these differences still persisted as long as two years after separation.

The much more severe ill-effects of total isolation (a very unbiological form of treatment) have been shown by Harlow and his co-workers (Harlow, 1958; Harlow and Griffin, 1965; Harlow and Harlow, 1969, 1970). Infant rhesus monkeys isolated for six months in early life showed gross and persistent disorders of social and sexual behaviour in adult life. These findings have been confirmed by other workers (Mason, 1960; Missakian, 1969).

Emotional behaviour is also markedly influenced by early isolation. Harlow's monkeys showed gross fear responses when first removed from isolation, and chimpanzees reared in a restricted environment showed avoidance of novel objects (Menzel, 1964). Dogs given restricted rearing exhibited increased activity and arousal and were slow to learn how to avoid painful stimuli, such as burns and electric shock (Melzack and Scott, 1957; Thompson and Melzack, 1956). To what extent the restricted rearing led to *deviant* behaviour rather than just impaired learning is uncertain. Melzack (1965) has suggested that restriction has the effect of increasing the novelty of cues in any testing situation (because of the restriction, stimuli which would be familiar to a normal animal are strange to a restricted one) and that this accounts for some of the apparently abnormal behaviour.

One important feature of restricted rearing procedures is the complexity of the resulting defects, so that it may be quite difficult to disentangle which element of restriction leads to which outcome by which mechanism. This is well demonstrated by the experiments on the effects of rearing animals (mainly cats) in darkness or in the absence of patterned vision (Ganz, 1968; Lindsley and Riesen, 1968; Riesen, 1965). This results in increased fear of new situations, deficiency in problem solving and other 'intellectual' tasks, perceptual deficits, retinal defects and dysfunction of the visual cortex. These studies emphasize that not only is 'behaviour' dependent upon experience for its development, but also that sensory stimulation influences neural growth. It has been well shown that neural metabolism varies with the rate of stimulation and recent work has demonstrated ganglionic atrophy and a reduction in dendritic growth following light privation during the stage of active cell growth. Preliminary findings of experiments with rats suggest that, conversely, stimulation in infancy may lead to changes in brain chemistry and an increase in cortical weight (Rosenzweig, Bennett and Diamond, 1967; Rosenzweig, Krech, Bennett and Diamond, 1968).

The cortical dysfunction following visual privation probably stems from *disorganization* of function, as well as from disuse. Thus, Hubel and Wiesel (1965) found that effects similar to those obtained from eye-lid closure followed the production of an artificial squint. The same workers (Wiesel and Hubel, 1965a) also showed that in some respects the effects on kittens of binocular privation of vision were less severe than those of monocular visual privation. It was as if the ill-effects of closing one eye could be averted by closing the other.

There is ample evidence from animal studies that in certain circumstances early life experiences *can* have far-reaching effects. The findings are sufficiently striking to make it well worthwhile to search for the possible long-term consequences of 'maternal deprivation' in man.

Drawing on the findings of his own studies in rats, Denenberg (1969) has summarized the effects of early life experiences in terms of five principles: genetically based characters may be drastically modified by early experiences; early experiences have long-term consequences; early experiences are one major cause of individual differences; early experiencies have multiple effects; and the age when stimulation is administered is critical.

These statements appear well based and probably apply generally, not just to rats. However there is also the other side of the coin. It could equally well (and rightly) be claimed that an individual's mode of response to the environment is greatly influenced by his genetic make-up. Children respond selectively to stimuli in terms of their idiosyncratic and developmental characteristics – they are not passive recipients of stimuli.

Rather, they *elicit* responses from other people (Bell, 1971; Yarrow, 1968). Children's characteristics help determine how their parents respond to them (Bell, 1964, 1968, 1971; Cummings, Bayley and Rie, 1966; Levy, 1958; Yarrow, 1963) and to some extent it may be that one child in a family is deprived whereas others are not, just because of his particular personality attributes. As Berger and Passingham (1972) have recently pointed out in a thoughtful review of the topic, the importance of individual differences in response to deprivation has been widely underestimated and neglected.

The special importance of infancy

It is frequently thought that the infancy period has a special significance in development so that environmental influences in early life have an overriding effect on what happens later, regardless of later experiences. This claim has been disputed in several reviews and actually there is no evidence that environmental factors can *only* have a decisive influence in early childhood (Clarke, 1968; Stein and Susser, 1970; Stevenson, 1957).

Two issues arise in this connection: whether there are 'sensitive' periods during which the individual is more susceptible to a particular life experience and whether the effects of infantile experiences always predominate over the effects of experiences in later life.

The existence of 'sensitive' periods has been shown for a wide range of functions in many different animal species. The example of 'imprinting' in birds, already mentioned, is of course well known but there are many others. The effects of infantile 'stimulation' in rats and mice vary according to the age when stimulation is administered (Bell and Denenberg, 1963; Henderson, 1964; Levine, 1962); the cortical dysfunction following visual restriction in infancy does not occur following similar restriction in adult life (Wiesel and Hubel, 1963); social isolation of older chimpanzees does not have the devastating effect it does on infants (Davenport, Menzel and Rogers, 1966), and the disturbance following social isolation in dogs is greatest when isolation occurs during the four- to fourteen-week period (Scott and Fuller, 1965). The presence of similar 'sensitive' periods in man has not been shown but it may be accepted that they are likely to occur.

However, it is important to note that these periods are not innately fixed and absolute (hence the modern preference for the adjective 'sensitive' rather than 'critical'). The influence of environmental variables on the timing of the period for 'imprinting' has already been mentioned – similar effects may be seen with other 'sensitive' periods. For example, the influence of age on the response to infantile stimulation in rats is dependent on the intensity of stimulation (Denenberg and Kline, 1964; Nyman, 1967). It should be added that the existence of a 'sensitive' period may depend as much on age-related differences in general attributes, such as emotional responsivity, as on any specific tendency to respond to a particular stimulus (Fox and Stelzner, 1966).

With regard to the overriding importance of infantile experience, it is certainly true that *some* effects of early privation are extremely persistent and resistant to later influences. For example, cats subjected to early visual privation show little recovery later (Wiesel and Hubel, 1965b), and chimpanzees show only limited improvement after early social isolation (Turner, Davenport and Rogers, 1969). Nevertheless, it would be wrong to suppose that this is a general characteristic. The relative importance of early and of later influences depends on the type and severity of the life experience at each age, on the developmental function concerned and on the animal species. In many cases later experience can have a marked effect.

The importance of experience in adolescence is perhaps most convincingly demonstrated with 'imprinting' in domestic birds – as this is the phenomenon classically (though misleadingly) associated with permanent and irreversible effects. For example, Guiton (1966) reared domestic cocks in isolation from one another for the first forty-seven days of life and compared their development with that of communally reared cocks. Many of the isolated birds when first tested attempted to copulate with a stuffed yellow rubber glove rather than with another bird (the cocks had been fed during the imprinting period by an experimenter who always wore yellow rubber gloves), whereas the communally reared birds copulated with birds rather than gloves. Both groups were then reared in pens with females until adult and tested again. Now both groups copulated only with hens. Apparently the isolated birds, following their adolescent experience with other birds, lost their reaction to man, and more specifically to the yellow glove, and exhibited normal heterosexual behaviour.

Similarly, Klinghammer (1967; Klinghammer and Hess, 1964) found that doves if raised individually by people became attached to them and when adult would choose human beings as their sexual partners. Yet this preference gradually waned following contact with other doves and after some years other doves, rather than people, were chosen as mates. This reversibility of early sexual imprinting does not apply to all species – in some cases later experience seems to have little effect (Hinde, 1970). Although early life experiences *may* have a permanent influence, in some circumstances the results may be overruled by the effects of adolescent experience. There is no experimental evidence for the unique importance of early experience in determining later choice of a sex partner, as was claimed by Lorenz.

There are age-specific effects, and early learning will influence later learning. Because of its primacy early learning may in some ways disproportionately influence development. Yet it is essentially reversible and in some cases the effects of later experience will predominate. There can be no general rule. Whether or not 'maternal deprivation' in infancy has a long-term effect depends in large part on environmental conditions in later childhood.

Factors modifying long-term effects
Separation from parents

For simplicity, separation experiences can be considered under three headings: very brief separations as a consequence of maternal care being provided by several or many mother-figures, transient separations lasting at least several weeks and permanent separations.

Very brief associations associated with multiple mothering. In spite of claims in the past that the children of working mothers are likely to become delinquent or show psychiatric disorder, there is abundant evidence from numerous studies that this is not so (Burchinal and Rossman, 1961; Cartwright and Jefferys, 1958; Douglas, Ross and Simpson, 1968; Hoffman, 1963; Rutter, Tizard and Whitmore, 1970; Siegel and Haas, 1963; Stolz, 1960; West, 1969; Yarrow, 1961; Yudkin and Holme, 1963). Children do not suffer from having several mother-figures so long as stable relationships and good care are provided by each. Indeed some studies have shown that children of working mothers may even be *less* likely to become delinquent than children whose mothers stay at home. In these circumstances it seemed that the mother going out to work was a reflection of a generally high standard of family responsibility and care. Two provisos need to be made with respect to these studies. First, there has been little investigation of the effects of mothers starting work while their children are still infants, although such data as are available do not suggest any ill-effects. Second, a situation in which mother-figures keep changing so that the child does not have the opportunity of forming a relationship with any of them may well be harmful. Such unstable arrangements usually occur in association with poor-quality maternal care, so that it has not been possible to examine the effects of each independently (Moore, 1963, 1964).

Much the same can be said about the effects of day nurseries and crèches (as particular forms of care often used when mothers go out to work). Assertions in official reports (WHO Expert Committee on Mental Health, 1951) concerning their permanent ill-effects are quite unjustified. Day care need not necessarily interfere with the normal mother–child attachment (Caldwell, Wright, Honig and Tannenbaum, 1970) and the available evidence gives no reason to suppose that the use of day nurseries has any long-term psychological or physical ill-effects (Yudkin and Holme, 1963). The one disadvantage of day-nursery care for very young children is that they get more of the common childish infectious diseases, presumably through their greater contact with other children and they tend to have more hospital care (Douglas and Bloomfield, 1958).

As has already been discussed so far as is known, there are no adverse psychological *sequelae* associated with upbringing in the Israeli kibbutzim, where children are raised in residential nurseries but still retain strong links with their parents (Irvine, 1966; Miller, 1969). Not only is their emotional development satisfactory but also the children do not appear to have the linguistic handicaps often associated with institutional care (Kohen-Raz, 1968). Anecdotal evidence has suggested that delinquency may actually be less frequent in kibbutzniks but enuresis may be more prevalent. Both these observations require systematic study before they can be accepted.

Transient separations. Several investigations of short-term separations (usually a month or more) in early childhood have shown little in the way of cognitive, emotional or behavioural ill-effects (Andry, 1960; Bowlby, Ainsworth, Boston and Rosenbluth, 1956; Douglas, Ross and Simpson, 1968; Naess, 1959, 1962) and rates of separation in child-guidance-clinic patients differ little from control populations (Howells and Layng, 1955). On the other hand, most studies have shown that children who experience separation from their parents for at least a month in the early years of life do have a very slightly increased risk of later psychological disturbance, particularly of an antisocial type (Ainsworth, 1962). The interpretation of this observation is bedevilled by the fact that in most studies widely differing types of separation experience have been pooled and in many cases the separation has also involved considerable deprivation or stress (Yarrow, 1964). Also, the children's subsequent experiences have frequently been atypical. Recent findings from our own studies show that separation is associated with antisocial disorder only when it occurs as a result of family stress or discord (Rutter, 1971a). Thus, children admitted for short periods into the care of a local authority show much deviance and disorder. But this is a group of children who have been at a social and biological disadvantage from birth (Mapstone, 1969), and their transient separation from home is but a minor episode in a long history of disturbing life experiences. Separations for other reasons (such as a holiday or admission to hospital) had no measurable ill-effects in our studies (Rutter, 1971a).

These studies have all been concerned with the emergence of *deviant* behaviour following separation and not with variations within the normal range. Evidence on lesser changes of a persistent kind following separation experiences is, however, available from Hinde's studies of rhesus monkeys. As already described, monkeys separated from their mothers for one week in infancy still showed more apprehension two years later in a strange situation than did non-separated controls. Although the behaviour of the two groups in a familiar setting showed no differences, this persisting difference in response to strange objects may well be of some importance. Whether or not similar changes may follow separation in humans is not known, but clinical anecdota suggest that *some* children may remain apprehensive of new situations for a while following an unpleasant separation experience. How often this occurs and how long it persists when it occurs is quite unknown.

Language retardation and intellectual impairment have not been a feature of separated children in any of the studies.

Prolonged or permanent separations. Similar problems arise in the analysis of the effects of very long-term separations which may also occur for a diversity of reasons. Thus, there is a very extensive literature showing an association between 'broken homes' and delinquency (e.g. Wootton, 1959; Yarrow, 1961, 1964), but no association with neurosis (Rutter, 1970; Wardle, 1961). However, in some cases the break-up of the home is no more than a minor episode in a long history of family discord and disruption, and to differentiate the effects of separation as such it is necessary to consider 'broken homes' according to the various causes of break.

The most obvious distinction is between homes broken by death and those broken by divorce or separation. It is only the latter which show a strong association with delinquency (Douglas, Ross and Simpson, 1968; Gibson, 1969; Gregory,

1965). Parental death has been associated with only a very slight (and usually statistically insignificant) rise in delinquency rate. Even this slight rise may not be due to the death itself (Birtchnell, 1969). Chronic physical illness which often precedes death is itself a factor associated with child psychiatric disorder (Rutter, 1966). Grief in the surviving parent is often quite prolonged (Bowlby and Parkes, 1970; Marris, 1958) and this, too, may affect the child's adjustment. Death of the father is frequently followed by economic and social deterioration (Douglas, Ross and Simpson, 1968; Rowntree, 1955) and these may also constitute important adverse influences on the child. Douglas, Ross and Simpson (1968) found intellectual impairment in bereaved children only when the death followed a prolonged illness.

Which parent dies seems of possible importance, in that two studies have found ill-effects to be most marked following the death of the same-sexed parent (Gregory, 1965; Rutter, 1966). However, this has not been found in other studies.

Because of the almost exclusive concern with 'maternal deprivation' there has been little investigation of the consequences of loss of a father. However, there have been some studies of the effects of paternal absence due to the father being away at sea, serving in the armed forces or absent for other reasons (Bach, 1946; Lynn and Sawrey, 1959; Sears, Pintler and Sears, 1946; Stolz *et al.*, 1954). The reports are few and the measures used were often weak, but it seems that serious disorders of behaviour were unusual. On the other hand it appears that in some cases the sexual identification of children is impaired by the continuous absence of their father (Biller, 1971).

Types of child care

The type and quality of child care provided has been shown to be a crucial factor in a wide variety of studies of both family settings and institutions.

So far as private homes are concerned, the most important variable with regard to behavioural development has usually been the quality of family relationships (Jonsson, 1967; McCord and McCord, 1959; Oleinick, Bahn, Eisenberg and

Lilienfeld, 1966; Rutter, 1971a). Parental discord, disharmony and quarrelling have been found to be associated with anti-social and delinquent behaviour in the children. Affectional relationships with the children are equally important and the degree of supervision exercised also appears relevant (Craig and Glick, 1965; Glueck and Glueck, 1962). In contrast, the methods of early child care (Caldwell, 1964) and the technique of discipline employed (Becker, 1964) seem to be of very little importance, except that extremes of discipline and great in-consistency are also associated with antisocial behaviour. No consistent associations have been found between patterns of care and neurotic disorders in the children.

In innumerable investigations low social class has been associated with poor intellectual and educational achieve-ment, which some studies have found becomes more marked as the children get older (Douglas, 1964; Ross and Simpson, 1971). Social class differences in patterns of communication have been found (Brandis and Henderson, 1970; Hess and Shipman, 1965; Robinson and Rackstraw, 1967), and it has been suggested that these are, at least in part, responsible for the poor cognitive performance of the children. However, so far, very little is known concerning parental influences on cog-nitive development (Freeberg and Payne, 1967). Brief pro-grammes of pre-school compensatory education have led to limited intellectual gains (Eisenberg, 1967; Klaus and Gray, 1968; Starr, 1971), but the variables which have led to cog-nitive improvement are not known.

Whereas numerous studies have documented the impaired language, poor intelligence and disturbed behaviour which frequently occur in children who have been reared in institu-tions (Ainsworth, 1962; Bowlby, 1951; Ferguson, 1966; Yarrow, 1961), this is found in children coming from only some institutions. Thus, Garvin and Sacks (1963) found an average *gain* of nearly nine IQ points in children admitted to an institution for short-term care (a period of some months) and Skeels (1966; Skeels and Dye, 1939) found a marked *rise* in IQ in children transferred from a poor overcrowded orphanage to an institution for the mentally subnormal where more personal care was possible. Gardner, Hawkes and Burchinal (1961) and Rheingold and Bayley (1959) found no emotional or cognitive deficits following institutional care. Du Pan and Roth (1955) and Klackenberg (1956) also found little intellectual deficit in young children in well-run institutions. These results stand in stark contrast to those of Dennis and Najarian (1957), Goldfarb (1943), Pringle and Bossio (1958a, 1958b), Provence and Lipton (1962) and others who reported gross intellectual impairment in institutional children. Similarly, Tizard (1971) found that children in residential nurseries had a normal intellectual level whereas Roudinesco and Appell (1950, 1951) found intellectual retardation to be prevalent.

It could be argued that these differences merely reflect differences in admission policy were it not for systematic experimental studies which have shown that change in institutional care can lead to an improvement in cognitive (verbal) level (Kirk, 1958; Lyle, 1960; Skeels, 1942; Tizard, 1964). But as many changes were introduced it is not possible to be sure which were responsible for the rise in intellectual level. The lack of adult–child interaction in institutions has been systematically assessed by Rheingold (1961); Provence and Lipton (1962) noted the inflexibility of institutional care; and David and Appell (1961) observed the lack of communication and responsiveness to the infants' needs. More recently, Tizard and his colleagues have done much to demonstrate the crucial features of institutional life and the ways in which various sorts of institutions differ one from another (King and Raynes, 1968; King, Raynes and Tizard, 1971; Tizard, 1969).

Some clues on the features likely to lead to retardation are provided by the experimental studies of the short-term effects of different types of stimulation (see page 39). Dennis (1960), in a comparison of institutions which led and those which did not lead to retardation, suggested that, at least for infants, lack of handling of the children, absence of toys and lack of play opportunities may retard motor development. The studies noted above have all demonstrated the lack of sensory, social and linguistic stimulation in many (but not all) long-stay institutions. However, to a considerable extent the answer to the key question of *which* institutional features lead to language deficit, intellectual retardation and behavioural disturbance remains a matter for further research.

Nevertheless, important clues are provided by animal studies. Stimulated by Hebb's (1949) theorizing on the importance of a diversity of experiences for intellectual growth, there has been a host of studies examining the effects of sensory restriction in infancy on later cognitive performance. Investigations using rats (e.g. Hymovitch, 1952; Nyman, 1967; Woods, Ruckelshaus and Bowling, 1960), dogs (e.g. Thompson and Heron, 1954) and chimpanzees (Davenport and Rogers, 1968; Rogers and Davenport, 1971) have all shown that a restricted rearing leads to later intellectual impairment, although Harlow, Schlitz and Harlow (1969) were unable to show this in rhesus monkeys.

Some progress has been made in specifying the crucial elements in early experience. Hebb's (1949) original pilot study compared laboratory-reared rats with those reared in his own home as pets and showed that the pets scored more highly on 'intelligence' tests and seemed better able to profit by new experiences at maturity. He suggested that the important difference between the groups was the greater breadth of experience of the pets who had been allowed to run about the house. This view has been substantially confirmed by later experiments (Bingham and Griffiths, 1952; Forgays and Forgays, 1952; Hymovitch, 1952). Rats reared in a 'free' environment giving access to a wide range of activities showed superior performance to those reared in individual cages. The importance of *breadth* of experience applies to sensory modalities as well as to range of activity. Thus, for example, Meier and McGee (1959) showed that rats reared with visual-tactile experiences showed superior perceptual abilities at maturity to rats reared with purely visual experiences. The same experiments have shown that it is indeed a range of perceptual and motor experiences which is crucial and not just the company of other rats. Thus, Hymovitch (1952) found that rats reared in individual mesh cages which were moved about the room from time to time were superior at problem solving to those reared in individual stove-pipe cages from which the animals could not see out. Similarly, Forgays and Forgays (1952) showed that among animals *all* of whom had been reared in a free environment with other animals, those brought up with playthings were better at problem solving than those brought up without playthings. Both seeing many things and doing many things had an important influence on intellectual growth.

While there are important differences with respect to the type of intellectual ability studied, it seems that for many skills active exploration of the environment influences development to a greater extent than purely passive exposure to sensory stimuli (see the experiments by Held and Hein discussed on page 55).

Although early life experiences may have a general effect on intellectual growth, the results of experiences in a particular modality are to some extent specific in nature. Accordingly, Forgus (1954) found that purely visual experiences in infancy were most important for later visual discrimination skills in rats, but that visuo-motor experiences were superior for the development of visuo-motor abilities (Forgus, 1955). Similarly, Nissen, Chow and Semmes (1951) showed that rearing a chimpanzee with its arms and legs enclosed in cardboard cylinders led to marked impairments in motor coordination and spatial orientation, but had no effect on visual discrimination. The specific effects on visual perception of early visual privation have already been described.

Human evidence is more limited, but what there is points in the same direction. White (1971) has found that providing babies with increased opportunities for touching things and looking at things led to an early maturation of certain visuo-motor skills. Starr (1971) reported an unpublished study by Saltz which showed that providing institutional children with a regular parent-surrogate aided their social adjustment, but did not influence intellectual development.

Undoubtedly the crucial difference between animals and man with respect to intellectual development is the influence of language on cognitive growth in humans. Verbal skills constitute a major part of intelligence in man and the presence of language aids intellectual growth in many ways (Rutter, 1972a). Here again specific influences are important (Rutter and Mittler, 1972) and the kinds of environmental conditions associated with the favourable development of verbal skills are not the same as those which foster perceptuo-motor development (Vernon, 1969). In short, although the evidence is incomplete and occasionally contradictory, it appears highly likely that different types of experience in early childhood are needed for different developmental functions. It is not possible to say which is the most important feature in child rearing. Rather it is necessary to discuss which experiences are necessary for which type of skill.

Little is known about the factors in institutional life associated with a better or worse social adjustment. Both Conway (1957) and Pringle (Pringle and Bossio, 1960; Pringle and Clifford, 1962) found that a stable relationship with an adult (not necessarily the parent) led to better adjustment. Similarly, Wolkind (1971) found less behavioural disturbance in institutional children when they had been at least two years with the same house-mother. This appears to be an important factor but without more and better information on other aspects of the children's life it is not possible to determine how important this factor is or what others may also be influential.

Duration of privation

If attention is confined to studies of institutions in which the children show adverse *sequelae*, most (Goldfarb 1943, 1947; Roudinesco and Appell, 1951; Skeels, Updegraff, Wellman and Williams, 1938) but not all (Dennis and Najarian, 1957; Pringle and Bossio, 1958a, 1958b) have shown that the longer the stay in the institution the greater the cognitive deficit and the greater the emotional and behavioural disturbance. Where negative results have been found, the care of older children has probably been superior to that given to the younger ones. Several studies have suggested that the children of mentally retarded parents have higher IQs if removed when young to a more intellectually stimulating home (e.g. McCandless,

1964). Not too much weight can be attached to any of the findings (positive or negative) in view of the uncertainties about the comparability of care at different ages and about the reasons why some children remained in care or with mentally retarded parents whereas others did not.

Nevertheless, it seems likely that the longer the privation persists the greater will be the psychological deficit in view of the similar findings from studies of children in their own homes (Gordon, 1923; Skeels and Fillmore, 1937; Wheeler, 1942). Older children in underprivileged homes were found to have lower IQs than the younger children. Conversely, Lee (1951) found that the longer black migrants from the South had had schooling in the (less depriving) North of the USA the higher was their IQ. There are important flaws in all of these studies either because the data are cross-sectional or because of the large number of children lost during follow-up. These flaws demand caution in accepting the results as they stand, but in the absence of better data it may be concluded that the weight of the evidence suggests that the longer the privation lasts the worse the effects.

Our own family studies (of children in their own homes) also provide circumstantial evidence in favour of this proposition (Rutter, 1971a). It was found that of children separated (temporarily) from their parents in early life because of family stress and discord, those who later were in a harmonious family setting were better adjusted than those who remained in a disturbed and quarrelsome home. Children whose parents had divorced or separated and whose *second* marriage was also disharmonious and unhappy more often showed anti-social behaviour than those whose parents were experiencing their *first* unsuccessful marriage. The presumption is that the marital discord had occupied more of the child's life in the former case.

Presence of good relationships

Mention has already been made of the evidence from Conway and Pringle that institutional children who maintained a stable relationship with some adult were better adjusted than those who did not. Our own findings with regard to children in their own homes produced similar results (Rutter, 1971a). In homes all of which were characterized by severe marital discord, fewer children who had a good relationship with one parent were antisocial compared with those who had poor relationships with both the mother and the father.

The opportunity to develop attachments with adults

Children admitted to institutions in infancy and who remain there until at least three years of age are in a situation less conducive to bond formation (see chapter 1) than are children in their own homes during this age period. Several studies have shown that the former is a group with a particularly poor outcome (Goldfarb, 1955; Pringle and Bossio, 1958a, 1958b). It also appears to be the group most likely to include children with the pattern of social disinhibition, indiscriminate friendships and an inability to form lasting relationships (Bowlby, 1946; Wolkind, 1971). In a study of foster care, Trasler (1960) found that prolonged institutional care in early life was the factor most likely to lead to subsequent breakdown of fostering. In keeping with the above suggestion, he also considered that this was the condition most likely to lead to affectionless detachment. The evidence on this issue is discussed in greater detail below when considering failure to develop bonds.

However, it should be added that institutional care at this age is perfectly compatible with a normal development of *language* and *intelligence* (Tizard, 1971).

Age of Child

Linguistic and intellectual retardation can arise with impaired life circumstances at any stage during the period of development, although the nature of the defects will vary with the child's age. Lack of vocalization, impaired responsiveness and developmental delay may be evident as early as the first few months of life in children reared in poor-quality institutions (Brodbeck and Irwin, 1946; Burlingham and Freud, 1944; Provence and Lipton, 1962). There is only very limited evidence on institutional effects on cognition and language in older children, but it appears that the older the child on admission the less the retardation (Pringle and Bossio, 1958a, 1958b). However, this finding is of little significance without evidence on the longitudinal course of cognitive development in children admitted to institutions at different ages – and this is still lacking. In view of the fact that post-natal brain growth is most rapid in the first two years of life (Marshall, 1968) and the probability that organisms are most susceptible to damage during periods of most rapid development (Dobbing, 1968), it is reasonable to suppose that the effects of privation might be most marked at this time. But evidence on this point is lacking. Furthermore, periods of susceptibility to damage should not be confused with periods when recovery can still occur (see page 75 for a discussion on this point).

There is some evidence that the long-term (delayed) effects of bereavement may be greatest in children whose parents die during the toddler age period (Rutter, 1966), but this point needs confirmation. There is also some suggestion that stress at this period may also be particularly likely to impair the acquisition of bladder control (Douglas and Turner, 1970). It is not known whether there is any period during the first five years when susceptibility to stress is particularly great.

Evidence on age differences in response to more long-standing influences such as parental discord or parental mental illness (Rutter, 1966, 1970, 1971a) is difficult to obtain just because the influences are chronic without any clear time demarcation. Nevertheless such information as is available suggests no particular age differences in susceptibility other than that young infants and older adolescents may be less often adversely affected.

Perhaps the one outcome which is crucially affected by age is the emergence of 'affectionless psychopathy', which appears to develop largely following lack of opportunities to form attachments during the first three years of life (this point is discussed in greater detail on pages 99 to 104).

Sex of child

Surprisingly little attention has been paid to sex differences in long-term responses to deprivation. Recent studies of the effects of family discord and disharmony indicate that boys may be more vulnerable to their ill-effects and there is some suggestion that this may also apply to other forms of deprivation (Rutter, 1970). The matter requires further investigation before firm conclusions are possible.

Temperament of child

The importance of individual differences was emphasized when considering the short-term effects of deprivation. Their relevance with respect to long-term effects can only be guessed at on the basis of their demonstrated influence in 'normal' children and in children whose parents have had some psychiatric disorder. The long-term consequences of temperamental differences in 'normal' children have been most systematically studied by Thomas and his associates in their New York sample of largely middle-class families (Thomas, Chess and Birch, 1968; Thomas *et al.*, 1963). They measured the behavioural styles of infants and young children and related these attributes to the later development of mild behavioural disorders. Emotionally intense children slow to adapt to new situations, irregular in their sleeping, eating and bowel habits who showed preponderantly negative mood were those most likely to develop behavioural disturbances a few years later (Rutter, Birch, Thomas and Chess, 1964). A child's own characteristics influenced the development of emotional and behavioural disorders. Circumstantial evidence suggested that they probably did so through effects on parent–child interaction (Thomas, Chess and Birch, 1968).

Rather similar attributes have been found to influence children's responses to the stresses associated with discord in families with a mentally ill parent (Rutter, 1971a). Children whose behaviour was difficult to change, who did not mind messiness and disorder and who were markedly irregular in their eating and sleeping patterns were significantly more likely than other children to develop deviant behaviours. Whether temperamental attributes are equally important in other types of privation or deprivation has not yet been studied, but research on this point should be rewarding.

Two questions arise concerning the influence of temperamental attributes. Are the attributes themselves a result of environmental influences or do they have an important genetic component? In so far as the attributes lead to deviant behaviour do they do so directly or rather by influencing the child's interaction with his environment? Only limited information is available regarding the first issue. Genetic aspects of these temperamental features have been little investigated (Rutter, Korn and Birch, 1963), but the available genetic studies of such attributes in children suggest an important hereditary component (Freedman and Keller, 1963; Scarr, 1969).

However, it should not be thought that these temperamental attributes are either immutable or entirely hereditary. Although continuities in development are present, considerable modification of individual attributes by life experiences can occur (Hertzig, Birch, Thomas and Mendez, 1968; Yando and Kagan, 1968). Furthermore, some individual differences influencing a child's response to the environment may be largely experiential in origin. For example, Zigler (1966) has suggested that a major component in institutional retardates' style of response to learning tasks is determined by their previous experiences of social reinforcement.

On the second question of the manner in which temperamental attributes influence development, it appears highly likely that the mechanism concerns the way in which such attributes influence children's interaction with the environment (Rutter, 1971a; Rutter *et al.*, 1964; Thomas, Chess and Birch, 1968). This is true of genetic influences generally – only rarely is a child psychiatric disorder inherited as such. One of the most important effects of genetics on behavioural development is through its influence on an individual's adaptability and response to stress (Glass, 1954; McClearn, 1970; Thompson and Grusec, 1970). This has been most clearly demonstrated in animal experiments showing, for example, the interaction of genetic differences (in maze performance) with environmental restriction and enrichment (Cooper and Zubek, 1958); genetic effects with respect to the pre-natal administration of adrenaline (Thompson and Olian, 1961) or other stress conditions (DeFries, 1964); and breed differences in dog's responses to 'indulgent' and 'strict' training regimens (Freedman, 1958). Genetic traits which give an advantage in one situation may lead to disadvantage in others (Searle, 1949).

Reversibility

The extent to which the ill-effects of 'maternal deprivation' are irreversible has always been one of the chief points of controversy. Bowlby's (1951) initial conclusion that mothering is almost useless if delayed until after the age of two and a half years and useless for most children if delayed until after twelve months has not been supported by subsequent research. The question now is not whether the effects are irreversible, but rather how readily and how completely reversible are the effects with respect to each function impaired by deprivation (Ainsworth, 1962). Evidence on these points remains limited.

With regard to the cognitive ill-effects of deprivation in childhood, there is probably some tendency to minor and partial remission with age in the normal course of events. Thus, the intellectual handicap at five to six years shown by the institutional children studied by Dennis and Najarian (1957) was less than the developmental retardation evident in the first year of life. However, this may be evidence that the circumstances were less depriving for older children than they were for infants. On the other hand, this could scarcely account for the IQ gains in adult life shown by the mildly retarded individuals from a socially deprived background studied by the Clarkes (Clarke, 1968) or those studied by Stein and Susser (1970). The observation that special training made little difference to the IQ gains (Clarke, Clarke and Reiman, 1958) suggests the operation of delayed maturation rather than a response to environmental change. These findings are of some interest, but it is important to recognize that the IQ gain with age was usually only moderate and fell very far short of reversing the early damage.

Considerable reversal of cognitive ill-effects is possible with a *complete and permanent change of environment*, provided that this occurs in infancy. This is clearly shown by the Iowa studies of children from very poor homes or inferior institutions who were adopted in the first two years of life (Skeels, 1966; Skeels and Harms, 1948; Skodak and Skeels, 1949). When tested in adolescence they had normal IQs which were some twenty or thirty points above that of their true parents. What is uncertain is the upper age limit beyond which complete reversal is not possible. Goldfarb (1955) found marked and persistent intellectual impairment in children transferred from a poor institution to a foster home at nearly four years. On the other hand, there is one well-documented case in the literature of a child reared in isolation with a mute mother in a dark attic up to the age of six years (Davis, 1947; Mason, 1942). When discovered she was severely retarded and without speech. Nevertheless, following intensive residential treatment she ultimately recovered to a remarkable extent, acquiring speech, gaining a normal intellectual level and achieving good social functioning. It may be concluded that extensive reversal is *usual* if the change of environment is complete and if it occurs during infancy. Reversal becomes less likely the longer the privation lasts and the older the child when removed from the privation. Even so, reversal may occasionally occur in older children.

These studies have sometimes led people to conclude that *partial and temporary changes of environment* might also have equally far-reaching effects, but the evidence shows that this is very far from the case. For example, the variety of studies of compensatory education for deprived pre-school children in the USA have demonstrated only modest short-term benefits (Eisenberg, 1967; Jensen, 1969; Klaus and Gray, 1968). What is surprising is not that the beneficial effects of six weeks' environmental enrichment proved transitory but rather that anyone supposed it would be otherwise. It is encouraging that such brief and partial enrichment had any effect at all, but it is evident that the ill-effects of long-standing and persisting privation cannot be corrected by short-term environmental tinkering followed by the child's return to the depriving circumstances.

The rather banal conclusion is that the degree of reversibility depends on the duration and severity of the privation, the age of the child when privation ceases and how complete is the change of environment. More precise specifications regarding these variables are not yet possible.

Less is known about the reversibility of growth deficits following privation. In general, when malnutrition is corrected there is a rapid acceleration in growth which to a considerable extent compensates for the previous retardation. However, the compensation is not usually complete (Birch and Gussow, 1970). Whether it is very nearly so or whether considerable deficit remains depends on both the duration and severity of the malnutrition and on the child's age at the time. So far, most of the follow-up studies of 'deprivation dwarfism' (see page 92) have been fairly short-term, but the results appear closely similar: that is, compensation is rapid but often not quite complete.

Very little information is available on the reversibility of the affectionless psychopathy syndrome. Whereas complete reversal readily occurs if privation ceases during the infancy period (as shown by the adoptive studies already mentioned) it is quite uncertain whether reversal can occur after two or three years of age. Clinical accounts suggest that reversal occurs only partially and with great difficulty after the infancy period, but systematic studies to support or refute that conclusion are lacking.

The persistence of the severe social defects in monkeys subjected by Harlow to total social isolation for the first six months of life may be relevant in this connection. As already noted, these monkeys were sexually incompetent, socially deviant to a severe degree and grossly incompetent as mothers (so that several of the first batch of infants were killed).

Some of these isolate mothers went on to have second and third babies and in a few cases mothering improved considerably (Harlow and Harlow, 1970). Harlow and Suomi (1971) have more recently tried to rehabilitate monkeys damaged by early total social isolation. Preliminary findings suggest that some of the damaged social capacities may improve appreciably given the appropriate social experiences after the infancy period. Even so, work with chimpanzees (Turner, Davenport and Rogers, 1969) suggests that the social abnormalities are modifiable only to a limited extent and then only with difficulty.

All in all, the scanty evidence available suggests that for affectionless psychopathy to be completely reversible, it is usually necessary for the child to have experienced normal relationships during early childhood. Data are lacking, but probably complete reversal is difficult after three years of age, although improvement may still occur later. Whereas antisocial disorder is certainly one of the most persistent of child psychiatric disorders (Robins, 1970), a change for the better in environmental circumstances during middle childhood was shown to be associated with a lower rate of disorder in our study of families showing discord and disharmony (Rutter, 1971a). Again, however, information is lacking on how early and how complete a change of environment is necessary for reversal to take place.

5 Long-Term Consequences: Possible Mechanisms

With respect to the long-term effects of 'maternal deprivation', mechanisms have to be determined for several distinct outcomes: mental retardation, dwarfism, delinquency, 'affectionless psychopathy' and possibly depression. It is clear from what has been said already that it is likely that the psychological processes involved in each of these are somewhat different.

Disruption of bonds or change of environment?

Whether the adverse effects of 'maternal deprivation' were due to disruption of bonds or a change of environment was an important issue with regard to the short-term effects, as already discussed. However, it is of less importance in connection with long-term effects in that admission to hospital (the situation where the issue arises most clearly) is of less consequence for long-term development. There is little association with delinquency and antisocial behaviour (Rutter, 1971a), mental retardation (Rutter, Tizard and Whitmore, 1970), 'affectionless psychopathy' (Bowlby *et al.*, 1956) or dwarfism (Patton and Gardner, 1963).

However, enuresis may constitute an exception in that recurrent hospital admission in the first four years does seem to be a factor leading to an increased rate of persistent bed-wetting (Douglas and Turner, 1970). In this case, the limited evidence available suggests that neither bond disruption nor change of environment is the most important variable. Whereas repeated hospital admission was associated with a slight increase in enuresis, much the most marked effect was seen with children who have some surgical operation. Burns and fractures were also associated with an increased

rate of enuresis. These findings from Douglas and his colleagues suggest that it is the presence of an unpleasant or
stressful experience which is influential rather than the separation from family or the strange environment as such. They
hypothesize that acute stress and anxiety during the first four
years of life may interfere with the normal acquisition of
bladder control. However, this may not be a sufficient explanation in that enuresis is also much commoner in children
from families where the mother has died or where the parents
have divorced (Douglas, 1970). The rate of enuresis is highest
of all where the children are placed in foster homes or institutions. Numbers were small, but contrary to the earlier
supposition, enuresis was most common when this occurred
at four to six years rather than before four years (Douglas,
1972). To what extent the bed-wetting is a function of family
discord that may precede institutional admission and to
what extent a consequence of an institutional upbringing is
uncertain. Douglas (1970) found that enuresis was just as
common when the mother had died as when the parents had
divorced or separated. This argues against the importance of
family discord as the main factor.

Enuresis is quite common in children in many kinds of
institutions (Stein and Susser, 1966, 1967). The evidence on
this occurrence suggests that enuresis is partly a result of the
stresses that led to institutional placement, but the finding that
enuresis among children in care is significantly commoner in
those in children's homes than in those in foster homes
suggests that the qualities of institutional life may themselves be important (although selective biases could also be
operative).

The one long-term outcome which may be associated with
disruption of bonds is depression (Rutter, 1971a). The evidence is somewhat contradictory but it appears that depressive
disorders during adult life may be particularly common when
a parent has died during the person's adolescence. This finding, if substantiated, refers of course to adult psychiatric disorder, which takes us outside the scope of the present review.
Depression in childhood has been less studied. One study

(Caplan and Douglas, 1969) linked loss of a parent with depressive disorder in children, but as the association was confined to children who had been placed in a foster home (it was not present in those losing a parent but remaining with the other parent), it is unlikely that bond disruption was the mechanism involved.

The evidence, then, from human studies suggests that although bond disruption is a potent source of short-term distress, it is not a particularly important factor in the development of serious long-term disturbance of any type. This conclusion seems at first sight to run counter to the findings from studies with subhuman primates, which show that even relatively short periods of separation from the mother are associated with measurable behavioural change in some (but not all) animals, certainly as long as six months, and probably two years later (Hinde and Spencer-Booth, 1971b; Spencer-Booth and Hinde, 1971b). In terms of the proportion of life-span this is equivalent to several years in humans.

This may be only an apparent difference in that the monkey studies were largely concerned with behavioural differences within the normal range and mostly in relation to responses to strange situations, rather than pathological outcomes. Even in humans, unhappy separations may sometimes lead to clinging behaviour lasting many months or even a year or so. These experiences may also render the child more likely to be distressed by separations when older. However, many children show *no* such long-term effects and even in those that do the effects are generally relatively minor.

To what extent there are real differences between man and monkey in the response to separation is not yet clear. The diminished activity and play found in monkeys five months after separation appears a greater effect than that usually seen in children after a comparable period of time, but comparative data are lacking. If it should turn out that there are differences, there are several possible explanations of why they might exist. In the first place, there are important neuropsychological differences between man and monkey (Drewe, Ettlinger, Milner and Passingham, 1970) and it is known that there are inter-species differences (perhaps between monkey and chimpanzee – Mason, Davenport and Menzel, 1968) in the response to various traumata. One mediating factor in this connection may be the presence of language. Although some extremely rudimentary features of language may be present in chimpanzees (Gardner and Gardner, 1969; Premack, 1971), language has not been demonstrated in monkeys. It may be that the opportunity to explain to children the nature of a separation experience makes it a less stressful experience than it would be without this possibility. Another possible factor is the nature of the care during separation. Unlike humans, other adult monkeys do not usually adequately take over the care of abandoned infants.* Although it is possible to ensure that all material needs are met during separation as before, nevertheless the infant's social experiences are quite different.

Whatever differences there may be between man and monkey, the available evidence from human studies suggests that mother–child separation in itself is not an important cause of *serious* long-term disorder. However, as we have already discussed with respect to short-term effects, separation experiences should not necessarily be equated with bond disruption. It may be that separation does not usually have long-term effects just because children can maintain bonds in a person's absence with the consequence that separation does not necessarily involve bond disruption.

Disruption of bonds or deprivation of stimulation?
Cognitive effects

The question of bond disruption or stimulus deprivation arises most clearly with respect to the effects of long-term institutional care. Numerous studies have shown that children reared in institutions are frequently retarded in language, general cognitive skills and scholastic attainment (Haywood,

---

* Although there is a shortage of good data on the point it seems that there are considerable inter-species differences in the behaviour of females towards young other than their own (Spencer-Booth, 1970). In many primates adult females do care for other young but, at least in the short-term, such care generally falls well short of that provided by the natural mother.

1967; Tizard, 1969). An institutional upbringing frequently involves both bond disruption and stimulus deprivation, so that in order to determine the psychological mechanisms involved it is necessary to seek situations where one occurs without the other.

First, we may consider what happens when there is bond disruption without stimulus deprivation. This probably occurs when a child loses a parent through death or divorce but remains at home with the rest of his family. Douglas's National Survey showed that parental death following an acute illness had no effect on intellectual development (Douglas, Ross and Simpson, 1968), Vernon (1969) found no association between 'broken homes' and intelligence, and the Isle of Wight study found no relationship between a 'broken home' and either intellectual retardation or reading retardation (Rutter, Tizard and Whitmore, 1970). Bond disruption, as such, is therefore not associated with mental subnormality or educational retardation. The fact that Bowlby and his colleagues (1956) found that children who had spent several years of their childhood in a TB sanatorium were of normal intelligence is also in keeping with this conclusion, although in this case it could just mean that the separation had not involved bond disruption.

If that conclusion is correct, institutions with a good level of cognitive 'stimulation' and adequate child care should *not* lead to intellectual impairment. That seems to be the case with respect to children reared in good-quality residential nurseries where there is plenty of staff–child interaction and stimulation but where relationships tend to be rather impersonal and where many adults look after each child (Tizard and Tizard, 1971). Such a setting would seem to involve little perceptual privation but might be likely to impede bond formation. The Tizards found that children in residential nurseries were more clinging and more fearful of strangers than children reared with their own families, but there was no intellectual or language retardation at three years (Tizard, 1971) and only very slight retardation at two years (Tizard and Joseph, 1970). It seems that it is not whether you are brought up at home or in an institution which matters for cognitive growth, but rather the type of care you receive.

Again, if that is so, it follows that if the quality of care is improved in institutions, intellectual and language development should improve even though the children remain separated from their parents. There is good evidence in support of this proposition. In one of the very early studies, Skeels and Dye (1939) reported a marked rise in cognitive level in a small group of children transferred from a very poor orphanage to a rather better subnormality hospital. McKinney and Keele (1963) found that increased physical attention led to more purposeful behaviour and verbal expression in severely retarded boys in a long-stay institution. Kirk (1958) showed that retarded children in an institution made significant gains in I Q (compared with contrast subjects) when given a special nursery-school programme. In the better controlled Brooklands experiment, Tizard and Lyle also found that the provision of better care for mentally subnormal children in hospital led to a significant gain in verbal development (Lyle, 1960; Tizard, 1964). Over an eighteen-month period the experimental group showed a ten-month gain on the verbal section of the Minnesota Pre-School Scale, compared with only four months for the matched control group. The exposure of children to environments differing in the range of environmental experience and amount of stimulation they provide can have an appreciable effect on mental growth (Stein and Susser, 1970).

The importance of stimulus deprivation rather than bond disruption is also shown by other findings. Douglas, Ross and Simpson (1968) found that children whose parent died after a chronic illness showed some intellectual impairment whereas those whose parent died after an acute illness did not. Presumably some aspect of child care was adversely affected by chronic parental illness, but the parental loss as such did not influence cognitive development. Secondly, many studies (Douglas, 1964; Douglas, Ross and Simpson, 1968; Nisbet, 1953a, 1953b) have shown that children in large families have a poor verbal intellectual development compared with children in small families. The effect seems to be environmental rather than genetic (Rutter and Mittler, 1972) and whereas the exact mechanism is not known, it clearly cannot involve bond disruption. Rather some aspect of parent–child interaction (probably involving communication) appears influential.

The same applies to children reared in homes which supply inadequate intellectual stimulation. Early studies of English gypsy and canal-boat children (Gaw, 1925; Gordon, 1923) and of children from isolated communities in the Kentucky (Asher, 1935) and Tennessee mountains (Wheeler, 1942) all showed that verbal abilities were seriously retarded, and were more so in older children than in youngsters, suggesting progressive impairment due to deprivation of some aspect of experience. Visuo-spatial abilities were much less impaired. Again bond disruption could not be involved.

The evidence all points to the conclusion that bond disruption *per se* has a negligible influence on intellectual development whereas lack of experience or stimulation has important deleterious effects on cognitive growth. The extensive animal evidence showing the importance of experience in the development of intelligence was discussed in chapter 3. Because the effects on cognition appear to be due to a *lack* of 'stimulation' rather than a *loss* of 'stimulation', privation is a more accurate term than deprivation.

Emotional and behavioural effects

The conclusion is different for the emotional and behavioural consequences of deprivation. Unlike the finding with regard to cognition, 'broken homes' *are* strongly associated with emotional and behavioural disturbance, particularly of an antisocial nature (Rutter, 1971a). Children not admitted to an institution but separated from a parent through parental divorce or separation have a much increased risk of delinquency. This is a circumstance involving bond disruption but probably not involving any alteration in the amount of stimulation. Accordingly, deprivation of stimulation can be ruled out as the effective mechanism. Whether bond disruption or rather distortion of relationships (either of which might be operative) is the relevant factor is considered below.

Very little is known about the emotional consequences of situations involving a lack of stimulation but no separation or bond disruption. There are well-established differences in the intellectual level of children from different social classes (Hess, 1970; Rutter, Tizard and Whitmore, 1970). These differences are probably partly genetic and partly environmental. In so far as they are environmental in origin, they presumably reflect differences in the type and quality of experience provided for the children. If stimulation differences were associated with emotional as well as cognitive effects, there should presumably be equally marked social-class differences in rates of psychiatric disturbance in childhood. However, this is not the case (Rutter, 1971a; Rutter, Tizard and Whitmore, 1970; Shepherd, Oppenheim and Mitchell, 1971).

In summary, bond disruption or some factor accompanying it is known to be associated with emotional and behavioural disturbance. The very limited available evidence suggests that pure perceptual restriction or poverty of stimulation has only limited long-term emotional consequences but considerable long-term effects on cognition.

'Sensory privation' or 'social privation'?

The conclusion that privation of stimulation has a deleterious effect on cognitive growth leads to the further question of what sort of 'stimulation' is important, and in particular, is it 'social stimulation' or 'sensory stimulation' which has the predominant effect? These are difficult to differentiate because in ordinary circumstances sensory stimuli are dispensed by people, with the consequence that if one is lacking so is the other.

Nevertheless, the distinction is a fundamental one which is of major importance in determining the direction of efforts to remedy the ill-effects of privation. The implications are most readily appreciated by contrasting the views of Casler (1961, 1968) and of Ainsworth (1962) with regard to the effects of institutional care. Casler has argued that what is crucial is the degree of stimulation and the range of experiences provided for the child. It is irrelevant whether or not these happen to be supplied by people, although in practice they usually are. Hence, his claim that 'the human organism does not need mother love' (Casler, 1968). On this basis presumably it should be possible to furnish the child with all that he needs by the utilization of robots which can speak (computers which can do just this, admittedly at a very primitive level, have already been developed), playthings and a rich and varied environment. In sharp contrast, Ainsworth (1962) has concluded that 'the deprivation offered by the institution chiefly stems from insufficiency of intimate interpersonal interaction'. She regarded perceptual stimulation as a merely incidental factor (at least over the age of six months), which had importance only in so far as this was provided by the mother. Accordingly, 'efforts to enrich the institutional environment by providing nursery-school experience seem to be less effective in stemming retardation of development than efforts to facilitate the attachment of the child to a substitute mother.' On the basis of Ainsworth's view, presumably, speaking robots, playthings and a rich and varied environment would be of negligible value in countering the intellectual impairment which occurs in many children reared in old-style institutions.

By polarizing views in this way it is possible that the argument has been taken a little further than Casler or Ainsworth intended by what they wrote. Even so, there is a very real and substantial difference in the way they view the effects of institutional care, which can be summarized in the distinction between 'sensory stimulation' and 'social stimulation' as the crucial elements.

The animal work showing the far-reaching effects of early sensory restriction in leading to intellectual impairment has already been discussed. Animals reared in enclosed cages with opaque sides were much inferior on problem solving to animals reared in a free environment. Because this difference involves both sensory and social restriction (the free environment allowed contact with other animals) it is necessary to look for experiments which differentiated between the two. As noted previously, rats reared in cages which limited vision were retarded compared with those reared in cages which allowed the sight of a varied environment, although in both cases there was no contact with other rats. Similarly, rats reared in a free environment showed a superior performance if there was ample provision of apparatus and playthings than if the room was barren, in spite of the fact that in both cases there was free contact with other rats. The conclusion must be that, in rats, changes in 'sensory' stimulation can influence 'intellectual' development even if there are no changes in social contact. It is not possible to say from the results to what extent 'social' stimulation is also beneficial. The fact that animals reared in a free environment were usually superior to caged animals regardless of apparatus provided might indicate the benefits of social contact or might merely mean that a free environment gave more sensory stimulation and a wider range of experiences.

There can be no directly comparable experiments with children and it cannot necessarily be assumed that what is important for rats is also important for humans. Yet what limited evidence there is suggests that 'sensory stimulation' also plays an important part in man's intellectual development. The benefits of pre-school compensatory education (Starr, 1971) point to this conclusion, as do the studies of the short-term effects of sensory privation and stimulation (see chapter 3). The fact that children reared in institutions which do not provide them with a regular mother-surrogate may have a normal level of intelligence is even stronger supporting evidence. The only direct comparison was undertaken by Brossard and Décarie (1971). They examined the effects on developmental quotient of extra perceptual stimulation (mobiles and tape-recorded sounds) and extra social stimulation (talking and playing with the baby) in two- to three-month-old physically normal infants in a large institution for babies born out of wedlock. The developmental progress of both groups was superior to that of a matched control group of unstimulated children in the same institution. But, up to the age of five months (the limit of the study), perceptual and social stimulation had the *same* beneficial effect. It seems clear then that in humans as well as in lower animals the range of activities and experiences in infancy affects intellectual development.

Much less is known about the relative importance of sensory and social stimulation with regard to *emotional* development. Certainly isolation in infancy has been shown to lead to later emotional disturbance in a wide range of species. Unfortunately, for present purposes, the environmental restriction in these studies involved both sensory and social privation and there are very few investigations which have separated the two. Mason (1968) has some preliminary findings which indicate that deprived monkeys are less fearful and more active if reared with moving dummies than if reared with stationary devices. Similarly, Sidowski (1970) found that physical restraint affected the social and play behaviour of isolated infant monkeys. However, not only are the findings tentative and in need of replication, but also they are concerned with medium and short-term social disturbances rather than long-term cognitive impairment.

So far in this section 'sensory stimulation' has been discussed as if it referred to a specific set of experiences, but of course it does not. The stimulation may involve different sensory modalities and it may be self-induced or the result of passive exposure. The animal studies described in chapter 4 made it clear that these differences matter. Different forms of stimulation are likely to have quite different effects on development. It is not that one form is more important than another, but rather that 'intelligence' involves many different skills each of which requires slightly differing early life experiences for optimal development.

A lack of visual, kinaesthetic or other perceptual experiences can and does impair intellectual growth in humans. Nevertheless, within English and white American cultures it has been found that environmental privation in childhood leads to a greater impairment of *verbal* intelligence than it does of visuospatial abilities (Haywood, 1967; Tizard, 1964, 1969).* This

* This may not be true of other cultures. For example, Jamaican children from an impoverished environment show a greater deficit on

suggests that one aspect of the importance of different types of stimulation may be gauged by examining environmental influences on the development of language and verbal intelligence. In considering human studies in this connection it is relevant that the intellectual effects of privation are similar for children reared in their own homes and for those brought up in institutions (Jones, 1954). This implies that the type of stimulation thought to be needed must apply both to institutions and to private homes.

Intellectual privation, apparently increasing with age, has been noted in canal-boat and gypsy children in England and in children from relatively isolated mountain communities in the USA (see page 85). Little is known of the way of life of these children but what evidence there is suggests that it is most unlikely that they suffered from lack of contact with people, in view of their close family life. In this respect, social privation appears an improbable explanation. Similarly, it seems dubious whether the canal-boat and mountain children suffered from a deficiency of sensory stimulation. On the other hand, the *quality* of the social contact (especially with respect to conversation) and the range and quality of sensory stimulation probably were restricted.

A similar impairment of verbal intelligence is found in children reared in large families (Douglas, 1964; Douglas, Ross and Simpson, 1968; Nisbet, 1953a, 1953b), and the evidence suggests that the mechanism is environmental rather than genetic in origin (Rutter and Mittler, 1972). Again, it appears highly unlikely that the children experience diminished social or sensory stimulation as measured in quantitative terms. Rather, it has been suggested that, because their contacts are more with other children than with adults, their language environment is less rich and less complex. However, it may be the *clarity* of the language environment, rather than its complexity, which is the key variable. Deutsch (1964) sug-

_____

certain non-verbal tests (Vernon, 1969). Whether this is due to a lack of important life experiences is not known. It could be due, for example, to malnutrition which is also often a feature of their early life.

gested that children's verbal intellectual development is impaired in homes where there is a predominance of meaningless noise over meaningful communication. In a study of tape-recordings of family conversations in the home, Friedlander (1971) found that the presence of children tends to lead to a tumultuous clamour in which several people speak at once on different topics. Perhaps, this kind of linguistic chaos makes language acquisition more difficult in large families.

Much the same conclusions stem from an examination of environmental influences on verbal development (Rutter and Mittler, 1972). Babies vocalize more if they are spoken to each time they make a noise. The presence of a non-speaking adult has little effect on vocalization, a tape-recorded voice markedly increases babble, but a somewhat greater effect is seen with a speaking person who is actually present in the room (Todd and Palmer, 1968; Weisberg, 1963). In other words, the main effect is produced by non-social verbal stimulation rather than by non-verbal social stimulation. On the other hand it is probably necessary for the verbal stimulation to be *meaningful* to the child. Mere repetition of words is not enough (Casler, 1965).

The same applies to effects on language development in older pre-school children (Brown, Cazden and Bellugi-Klima, 1969; Cazden, 1966). The provision of extra play sessions with toys has little effect unless there is also conversation with adults. But the special provision of sessions when adults deliberately engage the children in conversation has a significantly beneficial effect on language development.

Putting the evidence together, it may be concluded that the absolute restriction of sensory stimulation undoubtedly can impair development, including intellectual development. All forms of perceptual restriction may impede cognitive growth; different forms of restriction affect different intellectual skills. However, humans differ from animals in the additional, and crucial, importance of language with regard to intellectual development. Probably the single most crucial factor for the development of verbal intelligence is the quality of the child's language environment; how much he is talked to but more than that the richness of the conversational interchange he experiences. Because this must be meaningful to the child and because it is important that what the adult says develops and responds to the child's utterances, in all ordinary circumstances it is necessary for the verbal stimulation to be provided by people. However, several studies indicate that it is the conversation that matters, the mere presence of an interested adult is not enough in itself. Particularly in this connection, but probably in all forms of stimulation, the evidence suggests that it is the distinctiveness and meaningfulness of the stimuli which are more important than the absolute level of stimulation.

Emotional privation or nutritional privation?

The alternatives of emotional privation or nutritional privation largely arise with respect to the syndrome of 'deprivation dwarfism', a condition characterized by extremely short stature and (often) voracious appetite and marked delay in skeletal and sexual maturation, found in children who have experienced extreme and long-standing emotional and psychological deprivation (Patton and Gardner, 1963). Typically the children come from grossly disturbed families where they have been subjected to rejection, isolation and, in some cases, physical abuse; usually there is rapid weight gain following admission to hospital. Similar effects have been observed in children reared in poor-quality institutions (Fried and Mayer, 1948; Widdowson, 1951). The syndrome has become increasingly widely recognized in recent years and it has frequently been concluded that emotional deprivation leads to dwarfism even when nutritional intake remains adequate (Silver and Finkelstein, 1967).

The evidence for this view is circumstantial. Parents often report that the children eat large quantities (Silver and Finkelstein, 1967) and the improvement following removal from home suggests that the home circumstances have caused the dwarfing. Fried and Mayer (1948), in an early study, noted an association between growth rate and emotional adjustment in institutional children. They observed that the provision of an adequate diet did not improve growth until the emotional disorders had been corrected. However, there was no caloric control and no measurement of caloric intake. A study of orphanage children by Widdowson (1951) has been particularly influential. It was found that dietary supplements did not lead to weight gain in children in an orphanage with a harsh and unsympathetic supervisor. A difference in supervisor led to weight gain where the change in diet had not. Nutritional factors were carefully controlled so far as the food provided was concerned, but one may doubt whether food *intake* ran parallel. In the 'bad' orphanage it was said that when the supervisor had finished harassing the children 'the soup would be cold, all the children would be in a state of considerable agitation and several might be in tears'. Perhaps when they were so upset they left their food on the plate.

Several different mechanisms could operate to produce dwarfism. These include endocrine dysfunction, anorexia, distortion of diet, malabsorption and inadequate food intake.

In abnormal emotional states hypothalamic function may be depressed or cortisol secretion may increase (Powell, Brasel, Raiti and Blizzard, 1967), either of which could lead to impaired physical growth through hormonal mechanisms (Acheson, 1960). Powell, Brasel and Blizzard (1967) investigated thirteen children with short stature, polydipsia, polyphagia and who stole food. After hospital admission the behavioural abnormalities remitted and the children gained weight. The children came from very disturbed families and the growth retardation was attributed to emotional deprivation. Endocrine studies showed deficiences of A C T H and growth hormone in many of the children and the authors suggested that psychic disturbance had led to the hypothalamic dysfunction and so hypopituitarism. The significance of these endocrine findings remains uncertain in that other investigators have found normal steroid output (Silver and Finkelstein, 1967) and normal growth-hormone level (Apley, Davies, Davis and Silk, 1971) in children with deprivation dwarfism. It is possible that endocrine abnormalities are present in only some cases, but even when present it is uncertain whether they are the result of emotional deprivation or inadequate nutrition. That severe prolonged malnutrition (from any cause) can lead to a similar endocrine picture has been found in several studies (Powell *et al.*, 1967) so the endocrine dysfunction could be no more than a side-effect of malnutrition.

It is well recognized that affective disturbance can depress appetite and this could constitute the main effect of deprivation on growth, anorexia leading to impaired food intake. This could scarcely be the mechanism in the dwarfed children with voracious appetites, but some studies have reported that a number of 'deprivation dwarfs' have a low caloric intake and anorexia (Apley *et al.*, 1971; Talbot, Sobel, Burke, Lindemann and Kaufman, 1947). In these cases this could be the operative factor, as increasing growth seems to accompany rising food consumption.

In other cases there is also a qualitative deficiency of diet resulting from extreme food fads (Apley *et al.*, 1971). In this connection it is notable that feeding difficulties going back to infancy have often been reported (Silver and Finkelstein, 1967). These fads are only present in some children and it seems unlikely that the dietary distortion could be sufficient to account for growth failure, but it might constitute a contributory factor.

Another possibility is that changes in intestinal mobility, secretion and absorption might prevent proper assimilation of ingested food. Certainly, emotional factors can influence intestinal function as shown by experimental studies of individuals with a fistula (Beaumont, 1833; Engel, Reichsman and Segal, 1956). The presence of bulky offensive stools in some cases (Powell, Brasel and Blizzard, 1967) is in keeping with the concept of malabsorption, but where present this defect has not prevented rapid weight gain on hospital admission. This mechanism provides a feasible explanation but abnormalities of intestinal function have yet to be demonstrated in dwarfed children and clinical findings suggest that, even if found, malabsorption is unlikely to be more than of minor importance. Furthermore, it should be noted that early malnutrition may well be able itself to lead to later poor food utilization (Chow, Blackwell, Blackwell, Hou, Anilane and Sherwin, 1968).

Finally it could be that the deprived children are underfed in spite of parental reports to the contrary. A retrospective dietary history obtained from parents who may feel themselves subject to criticism is unlikely to be very accurate. The hypothesis of inadequate food intake has been tested in several experimental studies with results that support the view that this accounts for 'deprivation dwarfism'.

Normal weight gain was found in chimpanzees subjected to severe social isolation both in infancy (Davenport, Menzel and Rogers, 1961) and when older (Davenport, Menzel and Rogers, 1966). Similarly, Kerr, Chamove and Harlow (1969) showed that when infant rhesus monkeys were reared under conditions of total isolation but with normal opportunities for dietary intake, they developed gross behavioural abnormalities but their growth rates were entirely normal. In a study of three of these adult monkeys who had been subject to total social isolation in infancy, polyphagia and polydipsia were found (Miller, Caul and Mirsky, 1971), but this was apparently associated with no increased weight gain, so that some metabolic alteration may have occurred, even though there was no dwarfism.

Similarly, in deprived human infants growth retardation has not been found when the infants were adequately fed, as shown in a well-controlled study by Whitten and his colleagues (1969). Thirteen maternally deprived infants with height and weight below the third percentile were investigated. The inadequate mothering at home was simulated in hospital by solitary confinement for two weeks in a windowless room,* but the infants were offered a generous diet. In spite of the continuing emotional and sensory deprivation, eleven of the thirteen infants showed accelerated weight gain. The two others failed to eat properly although offered food. This

* This rather drastic treatment raises questions of how far it is justifiable to provide a restricted environment to human infants even for a brief period.

finding suggested that in most cases adequate calories is enough to reverse growth failure even when other types of deprivation persisted.

Following the period of understimulation the infants were given a high level of mothering and sensory stimulation, but the diet remained as before. This caused no change in rate of weight gain. The infants who gained during the period of understimulation continued to gain at the same rate and the two who did not gain in those circumstances still did not gain.

Following this study, three other infants were investigated. They were not admitted to hospital nor were the parents told of the suspected diagnosis of maternal deprivation. Instead, under the guise of investigation of caloric intake, feeding was carried out by mothers in the presence of an observer, no attempt being made to alter maternal handling or social circumstances. All infants gained weight at a markedly accelerated rate and the mothers subsequently admitted that the infants ate more food during the experimental period than previously although the diets were duplicates of what the mothers *claimed* they fed the infants. Other evidence also suggested that the mother's dietary histories were often grossly inaccurate.

The evidence from this study points strongly to the conclusion that nutritional privation is the crucial factor in dwarfism. Nevertheless the findings cannot be conclusive in that short-term weight gain was studied rather than long-term height gain and the infants were younger than most cases of 'deprivation dwarfism'. The Talbot study suggests that anorexia is important in some cases and the Miller investigation of isolated monkeys indicated that metabolic alterations may sometimes follow social isolation. In individual children a variety of mechanisms may operate (MacCarthy and Booth, 1970), but the balance of evidence suggests that, over all, impaired food intake is the most important factor. The impaired food intake may be due to either the child being given insufficient food or to his eating too little because of poor appetite. Emotional effects on metabolism or intestinal function remain theoretical possibilities, but there is no evidence that such mechanisms in fact operate to cause dwarfism, whereas there is good evidence that nutritional privation does occur.

Social privation or nutritional privation?

The alternatives of social privation or nutritional privation have to be considered with regard to the intellectual retardation found in children living in extremely poor circumstances. There is abundant evidence that mild mental retardation is extremely common among children brought up in city slums and rural poverty in the affluent countries of the world as well as in children living in poverty and social disadvantage in the emerging nations (Kushlik, 1968; Wortis, 1970). The hazards faced by children in these situations are multiple. Their mothers are likely to be in poor health, pre-natal care may be substandard and the children are likely to be delivered in unsatisfactory circumstances with increased risks of damage during pregnancy and the birth process. During their growing years the children are more liable to illness than their counterparts living in better conditions, more liable to malnutrition, more likely to live in disorganized overcrowded homes providing inadequate stimulation and educational opportunities, and are probably educated in poorly staffed, overcrowded, ill-endowed schools subject to high staff and child turnover. Each of these circumstances could lead to intellectual and educational handicap and the question arises which is the most important in this respect.

Intelligence develops and is not a 'given' capacity. Its development is a social process strictly dependent upon the quality and organization of the human environment in which it evolves (Eisenberg, 1969). That is not to deny that genetic factors play a major part in the development of intelligence. Indeed they do (Burt, 1958, 1966; Burt and Howard, 1957), but as geneticists have repeatedly emphasized, the aspects of behaviour that are polygenically inherited are not specific traits but patterns of growth and ways of responding to the environment (Dobzhansky, 1967).

Until recently most emphasis has been placed on the importance of social experience in intellectual development (Haywood, 1967). The evidence that experience and social stimulation are required for the development of intelligence has already been considered and there can be no doubt that social and linguistic privation in itself can and does lead to retardation of intelligence, particularly verbal intelligence.

However, it has become clear that this may not be the whole story. Firstly, it is well established that reproductive complications increase as one moves from more favoured to less favoured socio-economic groups (Birch and Gussow, 1970; Illsley and Kincaid, 1963), and the associations between perinatal damage, cerebral palsy and severe mental retardation have long been known (Illingworth, 1958; McDonald, 1967). More recently, Pasamanick and his colleagues (Pasamanick and Knobloch, 1961) have suggested that prematurity and perinatal complications may lead to lesser mental handicaps even when there is no overt neurological disorder – that there is a 'continuum of reproductive casualty'. The evidence on this point is difficult to interpret and to some extent contradictory (Douglas, 1960; Drillien, 1964; Harper and Wiener, 1965; McDonald, 1964). It is evident that some of the IQ differences associated with prematurity are accountable for in terms of social handicap, but it seems likely that even after the effects of social privation have been ironed out, some intellectual disadvantage may remain as a consequence of low birth weight (Birch and Gussow, 1970). In good social conditions the disadvantage is negligible or non-existent, but there seems to be an interaction effect so that the effects of low birth weight are greatest in deprived social circumstances. The biological handicap acts by lowering the organism's adaptability and increasing its vulnerability to environmental hazard. Even so, the effects of reproductive complications appear relatively small once the group with overt neurological disorder or severe mental retardation have been excluded.

The second possibility is that post-natal malnutrition leads to intellectual retardation. The evidence on this possibility has been reviewed by Birch and Gussow (1970), Cravioto, DeLicardie and Birch (1966), Stein and Kassab (1970) and in a series of papers in Scrimshaw and Gordon (1968). Nutritional privation in animals has resulted in a reduction in brain weight, histological and biochemical changes in the central nervous system, and behavioural deficits. These effects are probably most marked during the period of maximum brain growth (Dobbing, 1968). Thus, there can be no doubt that malnutrition during early development can damage the brain, but how marked an effect this has on intellectual development in the human is very difficult to assess. There are studies showing that children malnourished in infancy are often intellectually retarded when older. The difficulties in interpretation lie in the fact that undernourished infants almost always come from homes with gross social handicaps as well and it has not been possible to partition accurately the effects of social deprivation and malnutrition. This is particularly so as it is likely that only a small proportion of malnourished children come under medical care. This may account for Garrow and Pike's (1967) finding that Jamaican children admitted with Kwashiorkor in infancy were no shorter than their sibs at six to eight years of age.

In summary it seems that prematurity and pre-natal damage, post-natal malnutrition and social privation can all lead to intellectual retardation, and it is not possible at present to determine the relative influence of each factor. In any case the relative importance of each will be influenced by the particular social circumstances operating. In Britain it seems likely that social privation is the most influential factor, but the balance may be quite different in India or South America. It should also be added that the effects of each may well be different. Social privation (at least in an English or white American culture) probably has its main effect on language development and verbal intelligence whereas it is likely that both pre-natal damage and post-natal malnutrition cause a more global retardation of cognitive development.

Failure to form bonds or disruption of bonds?

Surprisingly little attention has been paid to this issue yet it is of great theoretical interest and practical importance. For example, it has extensive implications for the organization of institutional care for young children. If bond disruption is the damaging factor then it may be that institutional life should be so organized that none of the caretakers have sufficient intensive contact with the children for bonds to develop. If bonds are not formed then the children are less likely to suffer when the caretaker moves elsewhere leaving the child behind. On the other hand, if failure to form bonds is more deleterious, every effort should be made to ensure that the caretakers do have an intensive and stable interaction with individual children to encourage the development of attachments. If persisting bonds are developed with several caretakers, damage is less likely when one caretaker has to leave.

Unfortunately, there is very little evidence on this crucial issue. It should also be said that it is not necessarily a question of one alternative being worse than the other. Rather it may be that failure to form bonds and bond disruption have *different* effects. What little evidence is available supports this view.

To investigate the problem it is necessary to search for situations where the children will have had little or no opportunity to form stable bonds in early childhood. On the slender and incomplete findings available (see chapter 2) it may be postulated that bond formation is least likely to occur in a non-stimulating environment, where there is only low intensity of personal interaction, where infants tend to be left when they cry, where care is provided at routine times rather than in response to the infant's demands and where there are multiple caretakers none of whom have regular interaction with the child over a period of many months or longer. Such an environment is provided by the old-style large institution. Attachments normally develop during the first eighteen months of life, so that an institutional upbringing during the first two or three years of life is probably the single situation most likely to be associated with impaired bond formation.*

* But institutional care certainly cannot be the only cause of an 'affectionless character'. Lewis (1954), for example, in her study of 500 deprived children admitted into care found that only five of the nineteen children with this syndrome had suffered prolonged separation from their families.

Accordingly, failure to form bonds and bond disruption may be compared by contrasting children who enter institutions early in life and children who enter only after bonds have been formed.

Pringle and her colleagues investigated possible reasons for differences between stable and maladjusted children in long-term institutional care. They found that the stable children had almost always remained with their mothers until well after the first year and so had had the opportunity of forming bonds prior to admission. This suggests that failure to form bonds was most likely to lead to 'maladjustment'. The stable children had also more often experienced a dependable and lasting relationship with a parent or parent-substitute after going into care. In contrast, the maladjusted children had not had the same opportunity to establish or maintain stable bonds and their outstanding characteristic was an inability to make relationships with adults or children (Pringle and Bossio, 1960). Apparently, regular visiting by parents was often sufficient to maintain relationships while the children were in institutions (Pringle and Clifford, 1962).

In his study of working mothers, Moore (1963) found that the only group to suffer were the children who went from 'pillar to post' in a succession of unsatisfactory and unstable child-minding arrangements. In most cases these children had also had periods in institutions or residential nurseries. Their behaviour in early childhood was characteristically clinging, dependent and attention-seeking. In a more recent study, the Tizards (1971) found similarly that these were also the features which most clearly differentiated children in residential nurseries from those reared in their own homes.

Further evidence is provided by Wolkind's (1971) study of children in care. Psychiatric disturbance in these children took several forms, but the characteristics of indiscriminate friendliness and lack of social inhibition were especially a feature of children admitted before the age of two years. This suggests that failure to form bonds may lead not only to greater emotional disturbance, as suggested by the studies mentioned above, but also it may lead to a particular type of disturbance.

The special features of a failure to form bonds may also be examined by studying children reared in an institution from infancy and then comparing those placed in homes before three years when bonds may develop more readily and those not placed until after three years when bond formation may not occur for the first time so easily. This comparison was made by Goldfarb (1955), who found that although both groups showed emotional problems, those who remained in the institution until after age three years were especially characterized by an inability to keep rules, a lack of guilt, a craving for affection and an inability to make lasting relationships. They were also of lower intelligence and had poorer speech. The study is open to a number of criticisms in terms of the measures used and an uncertainty regarding the factors which determined whether the children stayed in the institution or were placed in foster homes. Nevertheless, for whatever reason, there were differences in the type of disturbance between the two groups; differences which may have been due to a failure to form bonds and differences which are strikingly similar to Bowlby's (1946) concept of 'affectionless character'.

In his study of forty-four thieves, Bowlby (1946) linked this inability to form relationships with separation experiences in early childhood. However, an examination of his case histories suggests that an affectionless character is associated not so much with a prolonged separation as with multiple changes of mother-figure or home in infancy or early childhood. This had occurred in seven out of fourteen affectionless characters, but only three of the other thirty thieves. It could well be that frequent changes of mother-figures during the period when attachments are normally formed could also impair bond formation. Two of the the other affectionless characters had spent nine months in hospital unvisited during their second year of life, when attachments would normally be consolidated.

It may be hypothesized on these findings that a failure to form bonds in early childhood is particularly associated with the later development of an 'affectionless character'. Can a disruption of bonds have the same effect? The studies already discussed imply that this outcome is only rarely a consequence of bond disruption. Follow-up studies of children admitted to institutions *after* the age when attachments develop confirm that affectionless psychopathy is *not* characteristic of children who have developed bonds and then had them broken or stressed by a prolonged separation. For example, this was not a feature of the children admitted to a T B sanatorium in Bowlby's study (Bowlby *et al.*, 1956), nor of children evacuated from London and placed in residential nurseries in Maas' study (1963).

No firm conclusions are yet possible from the patchy findings of these diverse studies. Nevertheless, the evidence does suggest that the effects of bond disruption and a failure to form bonds are different. It appears possible that a failure to form bonds in early childhood is particularly liable to lead to an initial phase of clinging, dependent behaviour, followed by attention-seeking, uninhibited, indiscriminate friendliness and finally a personality characterized by lack of guilt, an inability to keep rules and an inability to form lasting relationships. In contrast, this type of personality does *not* often follow bond disruption.

It may be thought that the clinging, dependent behaviour seen in young children is out of keeping with the failure to form relationships observed in later childhood. However, this is in keeping with cross-sectional age differences in the behaviour of institutional children (Dennis, 1960). There are no longitudinal studies in humans showing this progression, but this course of development is just what was found in Harlow's studies of monkeys reared in complete social isolation. As infants they clung to their mechanical mother-surrogates, sucked parts of their own body and were fearful in new situations. Later, they remained fearful, but also showed a striking deficiency in all forms of sexual, mothering and relationship behaviour (Harlow and Griffin, 1965; Harlow and Harlow, 1969, 1970).

It seems clear that experiences involving bond disruption do *not* normally lead to an 'affectionless character', but there are grounds for suggesting that a failure to form bonds in early childhood may have this outcome. This implies that there may be a sensitive period for the development of attachment behaviour after which bond formation becomes increasingly less likely. If such a period exists (and it has yet to be demonstrated) it begins about five or six months of age and it must last up to at least age two or three years in view of the usually good outcome of children placed in adoptive or foster homes at this age after early institutional care. The matter warrants further investigation.

Failure to form bonds or failure to form bonds with mother?

As a sub-issue on the question of the effects of failure of bond formation it may be asked whether the bonds have to be with the mother or whether any bonds serve the same purpose. In one of his earlier papers Harlow (1963) claimed that the mother–child affectional system differed qualitatively from other affectional systems, and observed that the clinging of monkeys reared only with peers differed from the attachment formed to the mother monkey. Clearly, there will be differences in the relationship as a function of the type of interaction – caretaking with the mother or play with peers. However the question is whether the bonds with peers or other adults serve the same function in psychological development as do the bonds with mother. The Harlow studies with rhesus monkeys suggest that in spite of differences at the outset, the long-term effects are remarkably similar (Harlow and Harlow, 1970). Few negative long-term effects have been found for monkeys reared with multiple-age mates but without a mother.

On the other hand, Bowlby (1969) still maintains that playmate relationships are quite different from attachments and he equates attachment with the mother-figure. Indeed mother is defined as 'the person who mothers the child and to whom he becomes attached'. However, Bowlby argues that social interaction is the most important part of mother-care and that feeding is not an essential part of mothering. If the essence of 'mothering' is no more than social interaction between the child and some adult it could well be suggested that the term has come to have such a wide application that it has ceased to have much meaning. Nevertheless, what evidence there is supports Bowlby's view that social interaction constitutes the basis of attachment behaviour (see chapter 2) and it is difficult to see what merit there is in tying the concept of attachment to motherhood if it is not necessarily tied to a female, not a function of feeding and only indirectly related to caretaking activities.

The factors leading to attachment listed above are ones which make it unlikely that in ordinary circumstances a child of the same age could provide what is needed for the development of a strong stable attachment. On the other hand, any adult or older child in close interaction with the infant could do so, whether or not he or she was a parent or caretaker.

Empirical findings on the benefits of bond formation with someone other than the mother are not available and this is an issue meriting much more study than it has received. However, there is Freud and Dann's (1951) classical study of six pre-school children who lost their parents as a result of Nazi persecution and who remained together as a group throughout a series of changes of concentration camps and thence to an English nursery. In these very abnormal circumstances the children developed unusually strong ties with each other and these seemed to have had a protective influence. While the children showed various emotional problems they did not show the gross disturbances which might be expected as a result of the total loss of mothering experiences and gross rejection that they had suffered.

There is no adequate evidence upon which to base any conclusions, but it may be suggested that for the development of social and emotional relationships in later childhood and adult life it is bond formation which matters and that it is of less consequence to whom the attachment is formed. In addition to this, caretaking and 'mothering' experiences are needed as are also play activities, but they serve a different role. Bonding, caretaking and play are three separate functions which may or may not be performed by the same person. It is hypothesized that so long as all three are available, it is of no matter, with regard to the prevention of 'affectionless psychopathy', who provides them, and in particular it does not matter if the mother does so.

That is not to say that it makes no difference in terms of individual psychological development with whom the young child forms bonds. A child, for example, who fails to develop a bond with his father or any other male figure in early childhood may not be able to make a really close relationship with him later. Although we still know little about the factors influencing psychosexual development, it is evident that early family relationships and attitudes are important (Rutter, 1971b). It may well be that youngsters who have developed bonds with adults of only one sex are at a disadvantage later with respect to heterosexual relationships and to the development of sex-appropriate attitudes and behaviour (Biller, 1971). It is probable that for optimal development bonds need to be formed with people of *both* sexes, and from what has been said about attachment behaviour it is very likely that early attachments will influence the kind of close relationships which are possible later.

Privation or deprivation?

As already discussed, the cognitive effects of inadequate stimulation are explicable in terms of privation (lack) rather than deprivation (loss). Similarly, the development of 'affectionless psychopathy' is probably due to a privation, rather than deprivation, of opportunity for bond formation. Deprivation has only seemed crucial with respect to long-term effects in the case of enuresis and stressful events in early childhood. However, surprisingly little attention has been paid in the literature to the distinction between not having some necessary experience as against having it but then losing it. The experience of loss appears important in the case of short-term effects of 'maternal deprivation'. The limited available evidence suggests that it is much less important for long-term consequences, but the issue requires further study.

As an extension of the concept of deprivation, there is the question of whether the most favoured children suffer more from loss than those already relatively deprived and so with less to lose. Gibson (1969) found that loss of a mother was more strongly associated with delinquency in families without social handicap, in keeping with the view that children with most to lose suffer more from loss. On the other hand, the reverse was true for fathers. In our studies (Rutter, 1971a), separation experiences were *only* associated with disturbance in children from *un*happy homes. Other investigations, too, have shown that the short-term effects of hospital admission tend to be worse for children with a poor relationship with their parents (see chapter 3). The evidence is most unsatisfactory, but on the whole it appears that children with the most favourable home environments are *least* affected by deprivation, and that those who have least to lose are most affected when they lose even that little. However, it is evident that the issue has been very little investigated and it remains quite possible that there is a form of long-term distress associated with deprivation or loss which differs from the results stemming from privation.

Disruption of bonds or distortion of relationships?

In an earlier section of this book the strong association between 'broken homes' and delinquency was noted. This association has commonly been held to demonstrate the seriously deleterious long-term effects of disruption of affectional bonds (Bowlby, 1968). The evidence on this point has been considered in detail elsewhere (Rutter, 1971a), but it may be briefly summarized here.

The main question is whether the harm comes from disruption of bonds or distortion of relationships. This may be considered by comparing homes broken by death (where relationships are likely to have been fairly normal prior to the break and where the bond is irrevocably disrupted) and homes broken by divorce or separation (where the break is likely to have been preceded by discord and quarrelling, or at least by a lack of warmth and affection, and yet where the break-up of the home may not necessarily disrupt the bonds). This comparison has been made in several independent studies (Brown, 1961; Douglas, Ross, Hammond and Mulligan, 1966; Gibson,

1969; Glueck and Glueck, 1950; Gregory, 1965). In each case the delinquency rate has been about double (compared to that for boys in intact homes) for boys whose parents had divorced or separated, whereas the delinquency rate has been only slightly (and non-significantly) raised for those who had lost a parent by death.

This suggests that it may be the discord and disharmony preceding the break (rather than the break itself) which led to the children developing antisocial behaviour. If that suggestion is correct parental discord should be associated with antisocial disorder in children even when the home is unbroken. There is good evidence from several studies (Craig and Glick, 1965; McCord and McCord, 1959; Tait and Hodges, 1962), including our own (Rutter, 1971a), that this is the case. In children from unbroken homes there was a strong association between parental marital disharmony and antisocial disorder in the sons. The McCords (1959) also showed that broken homes resulted in significantly less juvenile delinquency than did unbroken but quarrelsome and neglecting homes.

Delinquency is thus associated with breaks which follow parental discord, or discord without a break, but *not* with a break-up of the home as such. In fact, delinquency is *less* associated with parental death, with its necessary disruption of bonds, than it is with parental divorce, where bonds may still be maintained by intermittent contact after the break-up of the marriage. It may be concluded that it is distortion of relationships rather than bond disruption as such which causes the damage.

The same conclusion applies to temporary separations. In our own studies we examined the issue with respect to separations of at least one month's duration (Rutter, 1971a). There was no association between separation from one parent only and deviant behaviour in the children. There was an association between separation from *both* parents and antisocial disorder in the boys, but this applied only in homes where there was a very poor marriage relationship between the parents. Again this suggested that the association might not be due to the fact of separation from parents but rather to the discord and disturbance which surrounded the separation. To investigate this possibility separations were divided into those due to some event *not* associated with family discord (the child's admission to hospital for some physical illness, or a prolonged holiday) and those in which the separation was the result of family disorder or disharmony (usually break-up following a quarrel). Only when the separation was a consequence of family deviance was there an association with antisocial disorder (and in this case the association was strong). Transient separations as such are unrelated to the development of antisocial behaviour; they only appear to be so on occasions because separation often occurs as a result of family disturbance.

The issue was examined in a different way by Wardle (1961) who studied children attending a child-guidance clinic. He found that conduct disorder was not only associated with the child's coming from a broken home, but also with one *parent* coming from a broken home. The finding suggested that it was not the direct experience of bond disruption which mattered but rather the difficulties in interpersonal relations with which bond disruption was associated.

Little is known about the specific nature of disturbed relationships which tend to cause antisocial disorder in the children, but our studies provided some findings on this issue (Rutter, 1971a). Both active discord and lack of affection were associated with the development of antisocial disorder, but the combination of the two was particularly harmful. The longer the family discord lasted the greater the effect on the child, but the effects were not necessarily permanent. If the child later lived in a harmonious home the risk of antisocial disorder dropped. Whereas any type of prolonged family discord was associated with an increased risk of antisocial disorder, a good relationship with one parent went some way towards mitigating the harmful effect of a quarrelsome unhappy home. In short, the findings emphasized the importance of good relationships in personality development, but did not suggest that any one specific type of defect in relationship was of predominant importance.

Altogether the results strongly suggest that it is the *quality* of relationships which matter rather than the presence or absence of separations. It could still be argued that bond formation was nevertheless the crucial factor if (a) separations do not imply bond disruption and (b) if distorted relationships seriously impair bond formation. As already discussed, it is certainly unjustified to assume that separation is synonymous with bond disruption. In some circumstances children can maintain bonds through quite prolonged separations. On the other hand there is no evidence that distorted relationships lead to inadequate bonding. As Bowlby (1951, p. 69) observed: 'The attachment of children to parents who by all ordinary standards are very bad is a never-ceasing source of wonder to those who seek to help them.'

That is not to say that parental behaviour is irrelevant to the formation of attachments: on the contrary it plays a most important role. Among the factors thought to be important on the basis of systematic observations of infants are frequent and sustained physical contact, mother's ability to soothe her baby when distressed, her sensitivity to her baby's signals and the promptness with which she responds to his crying (Ainsworth and Bell, 1969; Ainsworth and Wittig, 1969; Schaffer and Emerson, 1964). These factors might well be influenced by parental pathology or parental discord. Yet it should be noted that, at least with younger children, maternal rebuffs and rejection seem to *increase*, not decrease, attachment behaviour (Bowlby, 1969). This observation is in keeping with animal studies. Scott (1963) found that puppies showed greater attachment (to the experimenter) when punished than when not. Similar results were obtained by Cairns (1966a, 1966b) with lambs. Harlow (Harlow, 1961; Rosenblum and Harlow, 1963) examined infant monkeys' attachment to a surrogate cloth 'mother' and found that a strong aversive stimulus from the surrogate (a blast of compressed air) only served to increase clinging behaviour. In the same way infant monkeys who were severely maltreated by their mothers nevertheless developed strong attachments to them (Harlow and Griffin, 1965; Seay, Alexander and Harlow, 1964).

It must be said that there is a lack of evidence on what happens in the long term to bonding in the presence of family discord and disharmony. Doubtless this depends among other thngis on the child's stage of development when rejection takes place. For example, it has been tentatively suggested that rejection very early in life may deter attachment, rejection at the period of most intense attachment behaviour may enhance it and rejection later when attachment is waning may encourage its dissolution (Rosenblum, 1971b). Whether this is so is not yet known. However, it certainly cannot be assumed that family deviance will necessarily lead to impaired bonding – indeed the animal evidence suggests that in some circumstances it might even lead to increased (although possibly less secure) bonding.

Part of the difficulty in successfully differentiating the effects of disruption of bonds and distortion of relationships is the fact that whereas the latter can be defined the former cannot, or at least has not yet been satisfactorily defined (Bowlby, 1969). That attachment behaviour occurs and is a crucial part of development is not in dispute. That bonds develop and are important is also not a matter for argument. The difficulty arises in differentiating approach (or attachment) behaviour from the existence of a persisting bond. This difficulty is multiplied many times when the existence of a bond has to be measured in the absence of the attachment figure, as is necessary to differentiate the effects of bond disruption from mere separation. The concept of bonds has proved useful in focusing attention on the minutiae of parent–child interaction, but it is important to remember that it is a concept (in the same way as 'drive' or 'instinct') and unless further specified does not provide an explanation. So far there is good evidence that disturbed relationships in the home are associated with the development of antisocial disorder in the children. As far as can be judged, this association cannot be explained in terms of bond disruption, but until a satisfactory operational definition can be provided for bond disruption it is not possible to take the matter any further.

Distortion of relationships or distortion of relationships with mother?

As the issue of deprivation has been discussed in the literature almost entirely in terms of *maternal* deprivation, it is necessary to ask if the harm to the child comes from distorted relationships in general, or specifically from a distorted relationship with mother. In our own study of family relationships it did not make much difference which parent the child got on well with so long as he got on well with one parent (Rutter, 1971a). Conversely, disturbed relationships with *either* parent led to an increased risk of antisocial disorder. Furthermore, disturbed relationships *between* the parents also put the child at risk. The Gluecks (1950, 1962) also found that affection and discipline from both mother and father were important factors in the genesis (or prevention) of delinquency.

Nevertheless, it would be wrong to assume that the mother and father had identical roles in the children's upbringing. In an earlier study it was found that boys were more likely to show psychiatric disorder if the father had died or if the father was mentally ill (Rutter, 1966). The apparent particular importance of the same-sexed parent also emerged in a study by Gregory (1965), which showed that delinquency rates were higher in boys if the father was absent from the home but in girls the rate was higher if the mother was missing. Thus, there are several studies which have shown the special role of the same-sexed parent. However, other studies (Gibson, 1969; Rutter, 1971a) have not found this and the matter remains unresolved at the moment. One suggestion is that the same-sexed parent is particularly important only at certain ages – perhaps in adolescence.

What is abundantly clear, however, is that it is not just the relationship with the mother that matters. It is true that mother generally has more contact with very young children and her influence on them often predominates (Wolff and Acton, 1968). On the other hand the father–child relationship is also important and sometimes it may even be the most influential (Bronfenbrenner, 1961; Peterson, Becker, Hellmer,

Shoemaker and Quay, 1959; Robins, 1966). Both parents influence their children's development and which parent is more important varies with the child's age, sex, temperament and environmental circumstances. Furthermore, it is not always meaningful to regard the influence of each parent as separate and independent. The mental health of one parent may influence that of the other (Kreitman, Collins. Nelson and Troop, 1970) and may also influence the marriage relationship (Barry, 1970). The family consists of individuals and pairs of individuals, but it is also a social group of its own and needs to be considered as such (Handel, 1968).

Distortion of relationships or deviant model?

Before concluding finally that it is the distortion of relationships as such which lead to antisocial behaviour in the children, three other possibilities have to be considered. First, there is a large body of experimental data which show how readily children imitate other people's behaviour and how a model of aggressive or deviant behaviour may influence the children to behave similarly (Bandura, 1969). These studies have been largely concerned with children's *immediate* response to an aggressive model, and the children's behaviour measured has mostly consisted of assertive or mildly aggressive behaviour within the range of normality. Nevertheless, it is quite possible that similar mechanisms might operate with more severe and more prolonged behavioural disturbances. Thus, it could be suggested that children in discordant families become antisocial, not because of any disturbance of relationships, but because they are following a deviant parental model of behaviour.

In keeping with this hypothesis is the fact that many of the parents in the most disturbed and unhappy families showed marked abnormalities of personality outside the family situation. Also in keeping with the hypothesis is our finding (Rutter, 1971a) that children are more likely to become antisocial when there is active discord in the home as well as a lack of warmth. On the other hand, there is a good deal of contrary evidence. Our own studies showed that parental personality disorder was *not* associated with antisocial disorder in the child unless there was also parental discord (Rutter, 1971a). Conversely, the adverse effect on the child of a very poor parental marriage was markedly ameliorated if the child had a good relationship with one parent. This is just what would be predicted if distorted relationships were what mattered. Contrariwise, given a quarrelsome home, if the child was only influenced by means of a parental model it should not make any difference if he happened to have a good relationship with one parent. West (1969) in his prospective study of city children produced similar findings. The characteristics of the family proved to be an important predictor of his later disturbed conduct and delinquency. However, once these family characteristics had been taken into account, the presence of a criminal parent did *not* add to the risk of delinquency.

In summary, the evidence is circumstantial but it points to the conclusion that distorted relationships are most important in the genesis of antisocial disorder, but that the presence of a deviant model may well be a contributory factor. Perhaps the best test would be what happens to children in a home which is without affection for the children but also without discord, deviant behaviour or criminality. The relationship hypothesis would predict delinquency in the children whereas the model hypothesis would not. Unfortunately, there are no satisfactory data on what happens to children in this situation. A follow-up study of children admitted in infancy to a well-run, harmonious institution, but one which did not provide close or affectionate relationships with the children, might provide the answer.

Distortion of relationships or ineffective discipline?

There is evidence from both retrospective and prospective studies that the parents of delinquent boys differ from other parents in their approach to the discipline and supervision of their children (Craig and Glick, 1965; Glueck and Gleuck, 1962; Sprott, Jephcott and Carter, 1955; West, 1969). It is possible that it is the child-rearing practices which matter in the genesis of delinquency and that the family discord is important only in so far as it is associated with erratic and deviant methods of bringing up children. This possibility could be tested only by some form of multivariate analysis in which the association of discipline with delinquency was examined after ironing out the effects of family discord, and vice versa. This has so far not been carried out in any of the published studies. It is hard to judge how likely it is that ineffective discipline could explain the findings. On the one hand there is little association in the normal range between methods of child rearing and child behaviour (Becker, 1964). On the other hand, associations at the extremes of a distribution often differ from those in the middle. The issue requires further study.

Nature or nurture?

One of the chief objections raised against the view that deprivation (in any of its forms) leads to adverse effects in children is that the association might well be explicable in genetic terms (Wootton, 1959, 1962). This objection could not apply to some of the varieties of deprivation discussed in this book, but it could apply to the association between distortion of relationships and the development of antisocial behaviour.

Before discussing the evidence on this point, it is necessary to make clear what is at issue. In the first place the question is not whether antisocial behaviour is due to heredity or environment. This is a nonsensical question as it must result from an interaction between the two. Secondly, the question is not whether *differences* between antisocial and other children are largely genetically or environmentally determined. This is a meaningful question, although it is always necessary to specify the environmental circumstances to which the answer applies.*
Rather, the question is very much more specific: that is, to what extent is the association between disturbed family relationships and antisocial behaviour genetically determined? It should be appreciated that it is quite possible for this

* Where environmental circumstances experienced by individuals are extremely different, the influence of genetic factors in accounting for individual differences will necessarily be less than when environmental circumstances are closely similar.

association to operate entirely through environmental influences and yet antisocial behaviour still have a strong genetic element (by virtue of other mechanisms).

The whole association could be accounted for in terms of heredity if a gene led to both delinquent behaviour and to personality difficulties giving rise to marital disharmony. In our own studies we found that within the group of families with a satisfactory marriage there was *no* association between parental personality disorder and antisocial disturbance in the children. This finding makes a genetic explanation less plausible, but a more direct test is offered by studies of adopted or foster children. When children are reared by their biological parents there is an association between parental criminality or alcoholism and deviant behaviour in the children (Jonsson, 1967; Nylander, 1960; Otterström, 1946; Robins, 1966). This does not appear to be the case to the same extent when the children are brought up away from their biological parents. Thus, in a recent Swedish study Bohman (1970) examined associations between deviant behaviour in adopted children and criminality or alcohol abuse in the true fathers (who of course had no contact with the children). No association was found. Similar results have come from less well-controlled studies. For example, Theis (1924) found little association between 'unsatisfactory' heredity in the biological parents and the social adjustment of their children who had been placed away from home. In a study of foster children, Roe and Burks (1945), too, found little difference between the adult outcome of those whose true parents were alcoholic and those whose biological parents were 'normal'. However, the offspring of alcoholic parents did have more serious difficulties of an antisocial type during adolescence.

There have been few twin studies of delinquents, but those that have been undertaken suggest that genetic factors play a relatively small part in the pathogenesis of delinquency and antisocial behaviour (Rosanoff, Handy and Plesset, 1941; Shields, 1954, 1968). The concordance rates are high in both monozygotic and dizygotic pairs and only slightly higher in the former.

The evidence is not very satisfactory, but it seems to show that the association between disturbed family relationships and antisocial behaviour in the children is environmentally determined to a considerable extent. However, studies do not differentiate between transient antisocial disturbance in childhood and the more severe delinquent disorders which frequently persist into adult life (Robins, 1970). It may well be that the genetic component differs in these two cases.

It should be added that the findings do not suggest that genetic factors play no part in delinquency. They probably are important with respect to the differences in temperamental features which render children more or less susceptible to psychological stress (see page 73).

Privation or stigma?

This book has been solely concerned with the effects of objective deprivation. It only remains to note that deprivation has a subjective side – the individual's view of his position relative to that of others whom he perceives as being better or less well off than himself (Eckland and Kent, 1968). By means of stigma, people may be socialized to disabling roles in life. It has been suggested that the effects of stigma may account for many of the consequences of socio-cultural deprivation, particularly when the deprivation is associated with membership of a minority or socially depressed racial group. Investigation of this issue is of the greatest social importance, but in the area of child development it is so far distinguished more by its promise than its achievements (Jessor and Richardson, 1968). There is some reason to suppose that an individual's immediate response in the test situation may be influenced by motivational factors associated with stigma (Deutsch, Katz and Jensen, 1968; Watson, 1970), but findings that similar effects may influence more long-term cognitive and educational progress (Rosenthal and Jacobson, 1968) have not been confirmed on replication (Claiborn, 1969). Even less is known about the emotional and behavioural effects of stigma. It could be that some of the consequences of 'maternal deprivation' discussed in this paper are attributable in part to the influence of stigma on social interaction, but this speculation remains a matter for further research.

Conclusions

In view of the many areas of research into 'deprivation' which lack sound data, it would be quite inappropriate to draw any firm conclusions at this stage. Interim conclusions of a tentative kind have been mentioned throughout the chapter, but the main findings can perhaps be drawn together by considering what mechanisms *might* underlie the main long-term consequences of 'maternal deprivation'.

A nutritional deficiency is probably the main factor responsible for the syndrome of 'deprivation dwarfism'. In parts of the world where malnutrition is rife it probably also plays a part in the genesis of mental retardation, but in Britain this is likely to be an uncommon occurrence.

A deficiency in 'stimulation' and necessary life experiences is likely to be largely responsible for those cases of intellectual retardation due to 'deprivation'. Perceptual privation is important in causing certain types of developmental and intellectual retardation, but humans differ from lower animals in the special role of language in intellectual development. Linguistic privation is probably most important in the poor vocalization of institutional infants and in the impairment of verbal intelligence seen in older children. In each case, although a certain minimum is required, the absolute amount of stimulation seems less important than the distinctiveness and meaningfulness of the stimulation to the child.

Distorted intra-familial relationships involving both lack of affection and hostility or discord are associated with the development of later antisocial behaviour and delinquency. Although the presence of a deviant parental model and inefficient discipline may be contributing factors, the lack of a stable, persistent, harmonious relationship with a parent appears to be the crucial variable.

Less is known about the syndrome of 'affectionless psychopathy', but the little evidence available suggests that the most tenable hypothesis is that a failure to develop attachments (or bonds) in early childhood is the main factor. A bond to one or other parent, usually the mother, is the strongest attachment formed by most normal young children. However, the evidence suggests that what is needed is a bond. Whether this is to the mother seems irrelevant in this connection and indeed it is doubtful whether it even has to be to an adult. Nevertheless, *which* person it is with whom bonds form is important for other reasons. Although the necessary facts are lacking it is probable that bonds with both men *and* women are advantageous for optimal psychosexual development.

Stress during the first six years (often but probably not necessarily involving parent–child separation) is a factor in the genesis of enuresis. However. some aspect of an institutional upbringing also appears important in that enuresis is common among children in a wide range of institutions. Which aspect of institutional care is pertinent in this connection is not known.

Loss of an attachment figure, although a major factor in the causation of short-term effects, seems of only minor importance with respect to long-term consequences, in spite of many previous claims to the contrary. Such a loss may play a part in enuresis, as one of several stress factors. Also, it may have a more specific connection with depression in adults. However, in this case the association is more with parental loss during adolescence than with loss in early childhood. Loss may be a minor contributory factor in other types of outcome, but so far as can be judged from the evidence it is not the main influence.

Indeed, the evidence strongly suggests that most of the long-term consequences are due to privation or lack of some kind, rather than to any type of loss. Accordingly the 'deprivation' half of the concept is somewhat misleading. The 'maternal' half of the concept is also inaccurate in that, with but few exceptions, the deleterious influences concern the care of the child or relationships with people rather than any specific defect of the mother.

6 Conclusions

It may be appropriate to end this reconsideration of 'maternal deprivation' by comparing the present state of knowledge with that extant at the time of Bowlby's review of the field in 1951. At that time there had been some fifteen years of research into the adverse effects of early deprivation of maternal care, but he was the first person to draw the strands together into one coherent argument. His report to the World Health Organization rightly became a most influential document, which stimulated a wealth of research and led to a reconsideration of the care provided for children being reared in institutions. Bowlby's exposure (by bringing together the results of a diverse range of reports) of 'the prevalence of deplorable patterns of institutional upbringing and of the crass indifference of certain hospitals to childish sensitivities' was likened in importance to Elizabeth Fry's exposure of the insanitary conditions in prisons in the nineteenth century (Wootton, 1962). His indictment of residential care of children led to a remarkable change in outlook that was followed by a widespread improvement in the institutional care of children.

On the other hand, his claim that maternal deprivation might have grave and far-reaching effects on a child's personality and intellect was met with considerable criticism and theoretical dispute. Several influential reviews pointed to the serious methodological deficiencies in many of the studies he cited. It was suggested that some of the supposed *sequelae* of deprivation might be merely artefacts consequent upon the biases existing in how children are chosen to be admitted to institutions, or might be due to hereditary conditions, or might represent the consequences of biological damage resulting from malnutrition, birth complications and the like. These criticisms were correct, but have not been discussed in this book as they have been amply documented by previous writers and because better controlled studies have replaced some of the weaker investigations upon which the 1951 report had to rely. Those faults in research design in the earlier investigations led, in some quarters, to a serious lack of appreciation of the importance of genetic and physical factors in children's development. It is necessary to redress the balance in this respect, as done in Berger and Passingham's (1972) review of 'deprivation'. Nevertheless, a parallel but opposite reliance on an outdated and incorrect deterministic view of development as a mere unfolding of hereditarily determined characteristics also requires redressing. It is fortunate that Bowlby's 1951 WHO report was immediately preceded by Hebb's (1949) classic, *The Organization of Behavior*, in which he outlined his ideas on the importance of experience in the development of intelligence. In the field of the study of animal behaviour this had as revolutionary an impact as Bowlby's book did on the world of child care. As a consequence, there is now a large body of animal evidence on the effects of early life experiences. These, together with a smaller group of well-controlled human studies, have amply demonstrated that early life experiences may have serious and lasting effects on development. This conclusion of Bowlby's which was regarded as very controversial twenty years ago is now generally accepted as true.

We may now take for granted

the extensive evidence that many children admitted to hospital or to a residential nursery show an immediate reaction of acute distress; that many infants show developmental retardation following admission to a poor-quality institution and may exhibit intellectual impairment if they remain there for a long time; that there is an association between delinquency and broken homes; that affectionless psychopathy sometimes follows multiple separation experiences and institutional care in early childhood; and that dwarfism is particularly seen in children from rejecting and affectionless homes (Rutter, 1972b).

Because this is widely accepted it is now possible to focus on the very important questions of *why* and *how* children are adversely affected by those experiences included under the term 'maternal deprivation', rather than spend time on *whether* they are affected. The diversity of experiences covered by 'maternal deprivation' was noted by Bowlby in his 1951 report and has been re-emphasized in numerous subsequent reviews. Nevertheless, the very existence of a single term, 'maternal deprivation', has had the most unfortunate consequence of implying one specific syndrome of unitary causation. This is apparent, for example, in Ainsworth's excellent and thoughtful reappraisal of the topic in 1962. Her whole review is explicitly based on the fact that 'maternal deprivation' covers a wide range of different experiences, but the unitary concept creeps back in her summary of findings (Ainsworth, 1962, p. 153) where the term 'deprivation' is repeatedly used as if it referred to a single stress. Manifestly it is not a single stress.

Twenty, and even ten, years ago there was a paucity of evidence upon which to base any analysis of the different mechanisms involved. Today things have moved forward somewhat and it has been possible to put forward some suggestions concerning possible psychological mechanisms. It has been hypothesized that the syndrome of acute distress is probably due in part to a disruption of the bonding process (not necessarily with the mother); developmental retardation and intellectual impairment are both a consequence of privation of perceptual and linguistic experience; dwarfism is usually due to nutritional privation; enuresis is sometimes a result of stressful experiences in the first five years; delinquency follows family discord; and psychopathy may be the end-product of a failure to develop bonds or attachments in the first three years of life. None of these suggestions has yet got firm and unequivocal empirical support and it is important to remember that they remain hypotheses which require rigorous testing. What is important is that it is now clear that the different elements in a child's early life experiences play quite different parts in the development process, so that the end-results of an insufficiency or distortion of each are equally dissimilar.

Throughout this book, reference has been made to age differences in children's responses to various forms of privation and deprivation. It has been apparent that these differ according to the type of life experience being considered. This reflects the important fact that children's needs differ according to their stage of development. No statement can be made about environmental influences without some specification of the age of child being discussed. This has been implicit in the whole of this account of 'maternal deprivation', but because of the lack of data on many aspects of age differences the effects have been discussed primarily in terms of different psychological mechanisms rather than in terms of developmental level. Nevertheless, in seeking to confirm or refute the hypotheses advanced it will be crucial to consider the effects in terms of how various experiences impinge on the developmental process.

Another problem in the use of the concept of 'maternal deprivation' stems from the actual words used. The term is misleading in that it appears that in most cases the deleterious influences are *not* specifically tied to the mother and are *not* due to deprivation (Rutter, 1972b). Reference to *The Shorter Oxford English Dictionary* shows that deprivation means 'dispossession' or 'loss'. While loss is probably an important factor in one of the syndromes associated with 'maternal deprivation', a review of the evidence suggests that in most cases the damage comes from 'lack' or 'distortion' of care rather than any form of 'loss'. Bowlby's claim in 1951 that 'mother-love in infancy and childhood is as important for mental health as are vitamins and proteins for physical health' was probably correct, but unfortunately it led some people (mistakenly) to place an almost mystical importance on the mother and to regard love as the only important element in child rearing. This is a nonsense and it has always been a *mis*-interpretation of what was said in the 1951 report. Nevertheless, this view has come to be widespread among those involved in child care.

Bowlby's own work in the last twenty years has gone a long way towards the specification of what are the crucial elements in 'mother-love'. His emphasis on the importance of attachment behaviour and on a young child's need to form lasting bonds with other people (Bowlby, 1969) has received increasing experimental support. This aspect of the mother–child relationship appears particularly important in connection with children's distress following certain kinds of separation experiences and with the (rather rare) syndrome of 'affectionless psychopathy'.

Nevertheless, some details of Bowlby's views on bonding have been questioned in this book. He has sometimes seemed to suggest that these two syndromes arise in a similar way, but the current evidence points to different mechanisms. Distress probably arises in part through *disruption* of bonds, whereas affectionless psychopathy probably arises because firm bonds *fail to develop*.

The whole notion of bonding also gives rise to some difficult questions. It is now clear that separation need not involve bond disruption and the two should not be regarded as synonymous. This assumption in the past led to a misleading emphasis on the supposedly deleterious effects of separation as such. This now appears incorrect and is one of the points on which the 1951 report needs major modification. Separation may or may not be harmful according to its effects on bonds and on attachment behaviour. It is the relationship itself which needs to be studied. But that raises another issue: if bonds can be maintained during a separation, then obviously bonds cannot be equated with attachment behaviour. But in that case how should one measure the strength of a bond (or even its presence) when the person with whom bonds have developed is absent? Further elucidation of the bonding process requires resolution of that difficulty.

A further point of departure from Bowlby's views concerns the supposedly special importance of the mother. He has argued that the child is innately monotropic and that the bond with the mother (or mother-surrogate) is different in kind from the bonds developed with others. The evidence on that point is unsatisfactory but what there is seems not to support that view. Two issues are involved. The first is whether or not the main bond differs from all others. It is suggested here that it does not. The chief bond is especially important because of its greater strength, but most children develop bonds with several people and it appears likely that these bonds are basically similar. The second concerns the assumption that the 'mother' or 'mother-surrogate' is the person to whom the child is necessarily most attached. Of course in most families the mother has most to do with the young child and as a consequence she is usually the person with whom the strongest bond is formed. But it should be appreciated that the chief bond need not be with a biological parent, it need not be with the chief caretaker and it need not be with a female.

Furthermore, it seems to be incorrect to regard the person with whom there is the main bond as necessarily and generally the most important person in the child's life. That person will be most important for some things but not for others. For some aspects of development the same-sexed parent seems to have a special role, for some the person who plays and talks most with the child and for others the person who feeds the child. The father, the mother, brothers and sisters, friends, school-teachers and others all have an impact on development, but their influence and importance differs for different aspects of development. A less exclusive focus on the mother is required. Children also have fathers!

The studies into the development of antisocial behaviour in children show the importance of family relationships. Discord, tension and lack of affection in the home all appear to increase the likelihood of the children showing disorders of conduct. The exact mechanisms involved remain unclear, but it seems that father–mother and parent–child relationships are both influential, and that this effect is not necessarily associated with defects in attachment behaviour. Distorted relationships rather than weak bonds seem to be responsible. This effect, unlike some of the others, is not one particularly associated with influences in early childhood and it serves to emphasize the importance of life experiences in middle childhood for some aspects of development.

Adult disorders have not been considered in this book, but later childhood and adolescence may be especially important periods for the genesis of depression, one of the psychiatric conditions in adult life associated with 'maternal deprivation'. Depression is probably particularly associated with being orphaned during early adolescence (Hill, 1972). It is likely that the mechanisms involved are multiple, but this may constitute another example of the effects of disruption of bonds. In keeping with this view (Bowlby, 1968; Bowlby and Parkes, 1970) is the fact that depression and suicide are associated with recent bereavement (Bunch, 1972; Parkes, 1964, 1965), with divorce or separation (Barraclough and Nelson, 1972) and with moving to a new neighbourhood (Sainsbury, 1972). Whether these associations reflect the same or different mechanisms should be further investigated.

Quite apart from 'love' and harmonious family relationships other features of the environment greatly influence children's development. This is most clearly evident with regard to intellectual development where experience with different forms of perception and of perceptuo-motor activity has been shown to influence later skills in perceptual discrimination and problem solving, which constitute important elements in the group of abilities called 'intelligence'. Animal studies show that although there are general effects, to a considerable extent effects are specific. The more limited human evidence is in keeping with this suggestion. Thus, visual experience is particularly important in the development of visual discrimination skills, experience of movement in the development of coordination, and so forth. However, human development differs from that in other animals in one key respect – the role of language. Verbal skills are an important part of 'intelligence' in man and those aspects of the environment which influence language are thereby especially important. It is in this connection that the amount, type and clarity of conversation experienced by the child is most influential.

The appreciation today of the importance of these perceptual and linguistic experiences in development departs from Ainsworth's conclusions in 1962 and differs from Bowlby's emphasis in 1951.

Feeding was at one time given a disproportionate role in child development by theorists. Hunger was seen as the source of 'drive' and activity and the relief of hunger was seen as the chief reason why children became attached to their parents – the theory of 'cupboard love'. These views have been shown to be largely mistaken (Bowlby, 1969), but there is a danger now of overlooking the importance of nutrition in other ways. The evidence suggests that privation of food may be an important cause of dwarfism in children from rejecting and neglectful homes, and chronic malnutrition may also sometimes lead to mental retardation.

Perhaps the most important recent development in 'maternal deprivation' research has been the emphasis on individual differences in children's responses to 'deprivation'. That some children are damaged and some escape damage has long been observed, but the differences in vulnerability have been regarded as largely inexplicable (Ainsworth, 1962). At last, some reasons are emerging for research. In the field of animal research, Hinde's studies of separation experiences in rhesus monkeys are most important in this respect. He has clearly shown that the mother–infant relationship *prior* to separation influences the infant's response to separation. This relationship is a reciprocal one and is influenced both by variables in the mother and variables in the child. The importance of child variables as determinants of mother–child interaction in humans has been emphasized by Bell (1968, 1971), and Graham and George's (1972) work examining differences in children's responses to parental illness has made an important beginning to the study of temperamental differences in children's reactions to stressful experiences. Much remains to be done, but what has been achieved so far shows that this is a fruitful field for study.

Curiously, one of the omissions until recently in this connection has been the study of sex differences. That boys and girls differ in their behaviour has long been known, but only in the last few years has attention been focused on sex differences in early mother–child interaction (Moss, 1967) and in responses to stress (Rutter, 1970). It is now evident that boys and girls do differ in these respects although exactly how they do remains ill-understood – another area requiring further research.

In a recent review of the effects of 'psychosocial deprivation' on human development in infancy (a topic closely related to 'maternal deprivation'), Bettye Caldwell (1970) suggested that three of the tasks requiring massive research efforts were: improved techniques of assessing the psychosocial environment, better measures of those aspects of human behaviour which react to changes of environment, and an exploration of the relationship between constitutional factors and the susceptibility to the influence of deprivation. Exactly the same applies to parent–child interaction and the effects of distortion, privation or deprivation of any kind of parental care.

The concept of 'maternal deprivation' has undoubtedly been useful in focusing attention on the sometimes grave consequences of deficient or disturbed care in early life. However, it is now evident that the experiences included under the term 'maternal deprivation' are too heterogeneous and the effects too varied for it to continue to have any usefulness. It has served its purpose and should now be abandoned. That 'bad' care of children in early life can have 'bad' effects, both short-term and long-term, can be accepted as proven. What is now needed is a more precise delineation of the different aspects of 'badness', together with an analysis of their separate effects and of the reasons why children differ in their responses. The chief purpose of this book has been to discuss some of the possible psychological mechanisms which might be investigated in this connection.

References

ACHESON, R. M. (1960), 'Effects of nutrition and disease on human growth', in J. M. Tanner (ed.), *Human Growth*, Pergamon.

AINSWORTH, M. D. (1962), 'The effects of maternal deprivation: a review of findings and controversy in the context of research strategy', in *Deprivation of Maternal Care: A Reassessment of its Effects*, World Health Organization, Geneva.

AINSWORTH, M. D. (1963), 'The development of infant–mother interaction among the Ganda', in B. M. Foss (ed.), *Determinants of Infant Behaviour*, vol. 2, Methuen.

AINSWORTH, M. D. (1964), 'Patterns of atttachment behaviour shown by the infant in interaction with his mother', *Merrill-Palmer Q.*, vol. 10, pp. 51–8.

AINSWORTH, M. D. (1969), 'Object relations, dependency and attachment: a theoretical review of the infant–mother relationship', *Child Devel.*, vol. 40, pp. 969–1025.

AINSWORTH, M. D., and BELL, S. M. (1969), 'Some contemporary patterns of mother–infant interaction in the feeding situation', in A. Ambrose (ed.), *Stimulation in Early Infancy*, Academic Press.

AINSWORTH, M. D., and WITTIG, B. A. (1969), 'Attachment and exploratory behaviour of one year olds in a strange situation', in B. M. Foss (ed.), *Determinants of Infant Behaviour*, vol. 4, Methuen.

ANDRY, R. G. (1960), *Delinquency and Parental Pathology*, Methuen.

APLEY, J., DAVIES, J., DAVIS, D. R., SILK, B. (1971), 'Non-physical causes of dwarfism', *Proc. Roy. Soc. Med.*, vol. 64, pp. 135–8.

ARSENIAN, J. M. (1943), 'Young children in an insecure situation', *J. abnorm. soc. Psychol.*, vol. 38, pp. 225–49.

ASHER, E. J. (1935), 'The inadequacy of current intelligence tests for testing Kentucky mountain children', *J. genet. Psychol.*, vol. 46, pp. 480–86.

BACH, G. R. (1946), 'Father-fantasies and father-typing in father-separated children', *Child Devel.*, vol. 17, pp. 63–80.

BAERS, M. (1954), 'Women workers and home responsibilities', *Int. Lab. Rev.*, vol. 69, pp. 338–55.

BAKWIN, H. (1949), 'Emotional deprivation in infants', *J. Pediat.*, vol. 35, pp. 512–21.

BANDURA, A. (1969), 'Social-learning theory of identificatory processes', in D. A. Goslin (ed.), *Handbook of Socialization Theory and Research,* Rand McNally.

BARNETT, S. A., and BURN, J. (1967), 'Early stimulation and maternal behaviour', *Nature,* vol. 213, pp. 150–52.

BARRACLOUGH, B., and NELSON, B. (1972), 'Marital relationships and health of spouse in relation to suicide', *J. psychosom. Res.,* in press.

BARRY, W. A. (1970), 'Marriage research and conflict: an integrative review', *Psychol. Bull.,* vol. 73, pp. 41–54.

BATESON, P. P. (1966), 'The characteristics and context of imprinting', *Biol. Rev.,* vol. 41, pp. 177–211.

BEAUMONT, W. (1833), *Experiment and Observations on the Gastric Juice and the Physiology of Digestion,* F. P. Allen, Plattsburg.

BECKER, W. C. (1964), 'Consequences of different kinds of parental discipline', in M. L. Hoffman and L. W. Hoffman (eds.), *Review of Child Development Research,* vol. 1, Russell Sage Foundation, New York.

BELL, R. Q. (1964), 'The effect on the family of a limitation in coping ability in a child: a research approach and a finding', *Merrill-Palmer Q.,* vol. 10, pp. 129–42.

BELL, R. Q. (1968), 'A reinterpretation of the direction of effects in studies of socialization', *Psychol. Rev.,* vol. 75, pp. 81–95.

BELL, R. Q. (1971), 'Stimulus control of parent or caretaker behaviour by offspring', *Devel. Psychol.,* vol. 4, pp. 63–72.

BELL, R. W., and DENENBERG, V. H. (1963), 'The interrelationships of shock and critical periods in infancy as they affect adult learning and activity', *Anim. Behav.,* vol. 11, pp. 21–7.

BENDER, L. (1947). 'Psychopathic behaviour disorders in children', in R. M. Lindner and R. V. Seliger (eds.), *Handbook of Correctional Psychology,* Philosophical Library, New York.

BERGER, M., and PASSINGHAM, R. E. (1972), 'Early experience and other environmental factors: an overview', in H. J. Eysenck (ed.), *Handbook of Abnormal Psychology,* 2nd edn, Pitman.

BERNSTEIN, B. (1961), 'Social class and linguistic development: a theory of social learning', in A. H. Halsey, J. Floud and C. A. Anderson (eds.), *Education, Economy and Society,* Free Press.

BERNSTEIN, B. (1965), 'A socio-linguistic approach to social learning', in J. Gould (ed.), *Social Science Survey,* Penguin.

BERNSTEIN, B. (ed.) (1972), *Class, Codes and Control: Applied Studies towards Sociology of Language,* Routledge & Kegan Paul.

BERNSTEIN, B., and YOUNG, D. (1967), 'Social class differences in conceptions of the uses of toys', *Sociology,* vol. 1, pp. 131–40.

BILLER, H. B. (1971), *Father, Child and Sex Role: Paternal Determinants of Personality Development*, Heath, Lexington.

BINGHAM, W. E., and GRIFFITHS, W. J. (1952), 'The effect of different environments during infancy on adult behaviour in the rat', *J. comp. physiol. Psychol.*, vol. 45, pp. 307–12.

BIRCH, H. G., and GUSSOW, J. D. (1970), *Disadvantaged Children: Health, Nutrition and School Failure*, Grune & Stratton.

BIRTCHNELL, J. (1969), 'The possible consequences of early parent death', *Brit. J. med. Psychol.*, vol. 42, pp. 1–12.

BOHMAN, M. (1970), *Adopted Children and Their Families: A Follow-Up Study of Adopted Children, Their Background, Environment and Adjustment*, Proprius, Stockholm.

BOWLBY, J. (1946), *Forty-Four Juvenile Thieves: Their Characters and Home-Life*, Baillère, Tindall & Cox.

BOWLBY, J. (1951), *Maternal Care and Mental Health*, World Health Organization, Geneva.

BOWLBY, J. (1958a), 'The nature of the child's tie to his mother', *Int. J. Psychoanal.*, vol. 39, pp. 350–73.

BOWLBY, J. (1958b), *Can I Leave My Baby?*, National Association for Mental Health.

BOWLBY, J. (1961), 'The Adolf Meyer lecture: childhood mourning and its implications for psychiatry', *Amer. J. Psychiat.*, vol. 188, pp. 481–97.

BOWLBY, J. (1962), 'Childhood bereavement and psychiatric illness', in D. Richter, J. M. Tanner, Lord Taylor and O. L. Zangwill (eds.), *Aspects of Psychiatric Research*, Oxford University Press.

BOWLBY, J. (1968), 'Effects on behaviour of disruptions of an affectual bond', in J. D. Thoday and A. S. Parkes (eds.), *Genetic and Environmental Influences on Behaviour*, Oliver & Boyd.

BOWLBY, J. (1969), *Attachment and Loss: I. Attachment*, Hogarth Press.

BOWLBY, J., and PARKES, C. D. (1970), 'Separation and loss within the family', in E. J. Anthony and C. M. Koupernik (eds.), *The Child in His Family*, Wiley.

BOWLBY, J., AINSWORTH, M. D., BOSTON, M., and ROSENBLUTH, D. (1956), 'The effects of mother–child separation: a follow-up study', *Brit. J. med. Psychol.*, vol. 29, pp. 211–47.

BRANDIS, B., and HENDERSON, D. (1970), *Social Class, Language and Communication*, Routledge & Kegan Paul.

BRIDGER, W. H., and BIRNS, B. (1968), 'Experience and temperament in human neonates', in G. Newton and S. Levine (eds.), *Early Experience and Behavior*, C. C. Thomas.

BRODBECK, A. J., and IRWIN, O. C. (1946), 'The speech behaviour of infants without families', *Child Devel.*, vol. 17, pp. 145–56.

BRONFENBRENNER, U. (1961), 'Some familial antecedents of responsibility and leadership in adolescents', in L. Petrullo and B. M. Bass (eds.), *Leadership and Interpersonal Behavior*, Holt, Rinehart & Winston.

BRONFENBRENNER, U. (1968), 'Early deprivation in mammals: a cross-species analysis', in G. Newton and S. Levine (eds.), *Early Experience and Behavior*, C. C. Thomas.

BROSSARD, M., and DÉCARIE, T. G. (1971), 'The effects of three kinds of perceptual-social stimulation on the development of institutionalized infants: preliminary report of a longitudinal study', *Early child Devel. Care*, vol. 1, pp. 211–30.

BROWN, F. (1961), 'Depression and childhood bereavement', *J. ment. Sci.*, vol. 107, pp. 754–77.

BROWN, G. W., and RUTTER, M. (1966), 'The measurement of family activities and relationships: a methodological study', *Hum. Rel.*, vol. 19, pp. 241–63.

BROWN, R., CAZDEN, C., and BELLUGI-KLIMA, U. (1969), 'The child's grammar from I to III', in J. P. Hill (ed.), *Minnesota Symposia on Child Psychology*, vol. 2, University of Minnesota.

BUNCH, J. (1972), 'Recent bereavement in relation to suicide', *J. psychosom. Res.*, in press.

BURCHINAL, L. G., and ROSSMAN, J. E. (1961), 'Relations among maternal employment indices and developmental characteristics of children', *Marr. fam. Living*, vol. 23, pp. 334–40.

BURLINGHAM, D., and FREUD, A. (1942), *Young Children in Wartime*, Allen & Unwin.

BURLINGHAM, D., and FREUD, A. (1944), *Infants without Families: The Case for and against Residental Nurseries*, Allen & Unwin.

BURT, C. (1958), 'The inheritance of mental ability', *Amer. Psychol.*, vol. 13, pp. 1–15.

BURT, C. (1966), 'The genetic determination of differences in intelligence: a study of monozygotic twins reared together and apart', *Brit. J. Psychol.*, vol. 57, pp. 137–53.

BURT, C., and HOWARD, M. (1957), 'The relative influence of heredity and environment on assessments of intelligence', *Brit. J. stat. Psychol.*, vol. 10, pp. 99–104.

CAIRNS, R. B. (1966a), 'Development, maintenance and extinction of social attachment behavior in sheep, *J. comp. physiol. Psychol.*, vol. 62, pp. 298–306.

CAIRNS, R. B. (1966b), 'The attachment behavior of mammals', *Psychol. Rev.*, vol. 73, pp. 409–26.

CALDWELL, B. M. (1962), 'Mother–infant interaction in monomatric and polymatric families', *Amer. J. Orthopsychiat.*, vol. 32, pp. 340–41.

CALDWELL, B. M. (1964), 'The effects of infant care', in M. L. Hoffman and L. W. Hoffman (eds.), *Review of Child Development Research*, vol. 1, Russell Sage Foundation, New York.

CALDWELL, B. M. (1970), 'The effects of psychosocial deprivation on human development in infancy', *Merrill-Palmer Q.*, vol. 16, pp. 260–77.

CALDWELL, B. M., WRIGHT, C. M., HONIG, A. C., and TANNENBAUM, J. (1970), 'Infant day care and attachment', *Amer. J. Orthopsychiat.*, vol. 40, pp. 397–412.

CAPLAN, M. G., and DOUGLAS, V. I. (1969), 'Incidence of parental loss in children with depressed mood', *J. child Psychol. Psychiat.*, vol. 10, pp. 225–32.

CARTWRIGHT, A., and JEFFERYS, M. (1958), 'Married women who work: their own and their children's health', *Brit. J. prev. soc. Med.*, vol. 12, pp. 159–71.

CASLER, L. (1961), 'Maternal deprivation: a critical review of the literature', *Monogr. Soc. Res. Child Devel.*, vol. 26, no. 2.

CASLER, L. (1965), 'The effects of supplementary verbal stimulation on a group of institutionalized infants', *J. child Psychol. Psychiat.*, vol. 6, pp. 19–27.

CASLER, L. (1968), 'Perceptual deprivation in institutional settings', in G. Newton and S. Levine (eds.), *Early Experience and Behavior*, C. C. Thomas.

CAZDEN, C. (1966), 'Subcultural differences in child language: an interdisciplinary review', *Merrill-Palmer Q.*, vol. 12, pp.185–219.

CHOW, B. F., BLACKWELL, R. Q., BLACKWELL, B. N., HOU, T. Y., ANILANE, J. K., and SHERWIN, R. W. (1968), 'Maternal nutrition and metabolism of the offspring: studies in rats and man', *Amer. J. pub. Health*, vol. 58, pp. 668–77.

CLAIBORN, W. L. (1969), 'Expectancy effects in the classroom: a failure to replicate', *J. educ. Psychol.*, vol. 60, pp. 377–83.

CLARKE, A. D. B. (1968), 'Problems in assessing the later effects of early experience', in E. Miller (ed.), *Foundations of Child Psychiatry*, Pergamon.

CLARKE, A. D. B., CLARKE, A. M., and REIMAN, S. (1958), 'Cognitive and social changes in the feeble-minded: three further studies', *Brit. J. Psychol.*, vol. 49, pp. 144–57.

CONWAY, E. S. (1957), 'The institutional care of children: a case history', unpublished Ph.D. thesis, University of London.

COOPER, R. M., and ZUBEK, J. P. (1958), 'Effects of enriched and restricted early environments on the learning ability of bright and dull rats', *Canad. J. Psychol.*, vol. 12, pp. 159–64.

CRAIG, M. M., and GLICK, S. J. (1965), *A Manual of Procedures for Application of the Glueck Prediction Table*, University of London Press.

CRAVIOTO, J., DELICARDIE, E. R., and BIRCH, H. G. (1966), 'Nutrition, growth and neurointegrative development: an experimental and ecologic study', *Pediatrics*, vol. 38 (suppl.), pp. 319–72.

CUMMINGS, S. T., BAYLEY, M. C., and RIE, H. E. (1966), 'Effects of the child's deficiency on the mother: a study of mothers of mentally retarded, chronically ill and neurotic children', *Amer. J. Orthopsychiat.*, vol. 36, pp. 595–608.

DAVENPORT, H. T., and WERRY, J. S. (1970), 'The effect of general anesthesia surgery and hospitalization upon the behaviour of children', *Amer. J. Orthopsychiat.*, vol. 40, pp. 806–24.

DAVENPORT, R. K., and ROGERS, C. M. (1968), 'Intellectual performance of differentially reared chimpanzees: I. Delayed response', *Amer. J. ment. Def.*, vol. 72, pp. 674–80.

DAVENPORT, R. K., MENZEL, E. W., and ROGERS, C. M. (1961), 'Maternal care during infancy: its effect on weight gain and mortality in the chimpanzee', *Amer. J. Orthopsychiat.*, vol. 31, pp. 803–9.

DAVENPORT, R. K., MENZEL, E. W., and ROGERS, C. M. (1966), 'Effects of severe isolation on "normal" juvenile chimpanzees: health, weight gain and stereotyped behaviors', *Arch. gen. Psychiat.*, vol. 14, pp. 134–8.

DAVID, M., and APPELL, G. (1961), 'A study of nursing care and nurse–infant interaction: a report on the first half of an investigation', in B. M. Foss (ed.), *Determinants of Infant Behaviour*, vol. 1, Methuen.

DAVIS, K. (1947), 'Final note on a case of extreme isolation', *Amer. J. Sociol.*, vol. 52, pp. 432–7.

DEFRIES, J. C. (1964), 'Prenatal maternal stress in mice: differential effects on behaviour', *J. Hered.*, vol. 55, pp. 289–95.

DENENBERG, V. H. (1969), 'Animal studies of early experience: some principles which have implications for human development', in J. P. Hill (ed.), *Minnesota Symposia on Child Psychology*, vol. 3, University of Minnesota Press.

DENENBERG, V. H., and KLINE, N. J. (1964), 'Stimulus intensity vs critical periods: a test of two hypotheses concerning infantile stimulation', *Canad. J. Psychol.*, vol. 18, pp. 1–5.

DENNIS, W. (1960), 'Causes of retardation among institutional children: Iran', *J. genet. Psychol.*, vol. 96, pp.47–59.

DENNIS, W., and NAJARIAN, P. (1957), 'Infant development under environmental handicap', *Psychol. Monogr.*, vol. 71, pp. 1–13.

DEUTSCH, C. P. (1964), 'Auditory discrimination and learning: social factors', *Merrill-Palmer Q.*, vol. 10, pp. 277–96.

DEUTSCH, H. (1919), 'A two-year-old boy's first love comes to grief', in L. Jessner and E. Pavenstedt (eds.), *Dynamic Psychopathology in Childhood*, Grune & Stratton.

DEUTSCH, M., KATZ, I., and JENSEN, A. (eds.) (1968), *Social Class, Race and Psychological Development*, Holt, Rinehart & Winston.

DINNAGE, R., and PRINGLE, M. L. K. (1967a), *Residential Child Care: Facts and Fallacies*, Longman.

DINNAGE, R., and PRINGLE, M. L. K. (1967b), *Foster Home Care: Facts and Fallacies*, Longman.

DOBBING, J. (1968), 'Vulnerable periods in developing brain', in A. N. Davison and J. Dobbing (eds.), *Applied Neurochemistry*, Blackwell.

DOBZHANSKY, T. (1967), 'On types, genotypes and genetic diversity in populations', in J. N. Spuhler (ed.), *Genetic Diversity and Human Behavior*, Aldine.

DOUGLAS, J. W. B. (1960), 'Premature children at primary schools', *Brit. med. J.*, vol. 1, pp. 1008-13.

DOUGLAS, J. W. B. (1964), *The Home and the School*, MacGibbon & Kee.

DOUGLAS, J. W. B. (1970), 'Broken families and child behaviour', *J. Roy. Coll. Physns Lond.*, vol. 4, pp. 203-10.

DOUGLAS, J. W. B. (1972), 'Early psychological experiences and later enuresis', in I. Kolvin, R. MacKeith and R. Meadow (eds.), *Recent Advances in Bladder Control in Children*, Heinemann, in press.

DOUGLAS, J. W. B., and BLOMFIELD, J. M. (1958), *Children under Five*, Allen & Unwin.

DOUGLAS, J. W. B., and TURNER, R. K. (1970), 'The association of anxiety provoking events in early childhood with enuresis', *Proc. Fifth Int. Sci. Meeting of Int. Epid. Assn*, Savremena Adinistracija, Belgrade.

DOUGLAS, J. W. B., ROSS, J. M., and SIMPSON, H. R. (1968), *All Our Future: A Longitudinal Study of Secondary Education*, Peter Davies.

DOUGLAS, J. W. B., ROSS, J. M., HAMMOND, W. A., and MULLIGAN, D. G. (1966), 'Delinquency and social class', *Brit. J. Criminol.*, vol. 6, pp. 294-302.

DREWE, E. A., ETTLINGER, G., MILNER, A. D., and PASSINGHAM, R. E. (1970), 'A comparative review of the results of neuropsychological research on man and monkey', *Cortex*, vol. 6, pp. 129-63.

DRILLIEN, C. M. (1964), *Growth and Development of the Prematurely Born Infant*, Livingstone.

DU PAN, M., and ROTH, S. (1955), 'The psychologic development of a group of children brought up in a hospital type residential nursery', *J. Pediat.*, vol. 47, pp. 124-9.

ECKLAND, B., and KENT, D. P. (1968), 'Socialization and social structure', in *Perspectives on Human Deprivation: Biological, Psychological and Sociological*, US Department of Health, Education and Welfare.

EISENBERG, L. (1967), 'Clinical considerations in the
psychiatric evaluation of intelligence', in J. Zubin and
G. A. Jervis (eds.), *Psychopathology of Mental Development*,
Grune & Stratton.

EISENBERG, L. (1969), 'The social development of intelligence',
in H. Freeman (ed.), *Progress in Mental Health*, Churchill.

ENGEL, G. L., REICHSMAN, F., and SEGAL, H. (1956),
'A study of an infant with gastric fistula: I. Behavior and the rate
of total hydrochloric acid secretion', *Psychosom. Med.*, vol. 18,
pp. 374–98.

FABRICIUS, E. (1962), 'Some aspects of imprinting in birds',
Symp. Zool. Soc. Lond., vol. 8, pp. 139–48.

FAGIN, C. M. R. N. (1966), *The Effects of Maternal Attendance
during Hospitalization on the Post-Hospital Behavior of Young
Children: A Comparative Study*, F. A. Davis.

FAUST, O. A., JACKSON, K., CERMAK, E. G., BURTT, M. M.,
and WINKLEY, R. (1952), *Reducing Emotional Trauma in
Hospitalized Children*, Albany Research Project, Albany, New York.

FERGUSON, T. (1966), *Children in Care – and After*, Oxford
University Press.

FORGAYS, D. G., and FORGAYS, J. W. (1952), 'The nature of the
effect of free-environmental experience in the rat', *J. comp. physiol.
Psychol.*, vol. 45, pp. 322–8.

FORGUS, R. H. (1954), 'The effects of early perceptual learning
on the behavioral organization of adult rats', *J. comp. physiol.
Psychol.*, vol. 47, pp. 331–6.

FORGUS, R. H. (1955), 'Influence of early experience on
maze-learning with and without visual cues', *Canad. J. Psychol.*,
vol. 9, pp. 207–14.

FOX, M. W., and STELZNER, D. (1966), 'Approach/withdrawal
variables in the development of social behaviour in the dog',
Anim. Behav., vol. 14, pp. 362–6.

FRANCIS, S. H. (1971), 'The effects of own-home and institution
rearing on the behavioral development of normal and mongol
children', *J. child Psychol. Psychiat.*, vol. 12, pp. 173–90.

FREEBERG, N. E., and PAYNE, D. T. (1967), 'Parental influence on
cognitive development in early childhood: a review', *Child Devel.*,
vol. 38, pp. 65–87.

FREEDMAN, D. G. (1958), 'Constitutional and environmental
interactions in rearing of four breeds of dog', *Science*,
vol. 127, pp. 585–6.

FREEDMAN, D. G. (1965), 'Hereditary control of early social
behaviour', in B. M. Foss (ed.), *Determinants of Infant Behaviour*,
vol. 3, Methuen.

FREEDMAN, D. G., and KELLER, B. (1963), 'Inheritance of
behaviour in infants', *Science*, vol. 140, pp. 196–8.

FREUD, A., and DANN, S. (1951), 'An experiment in group upbringing', *Psychoanal. Stud. Child*, vol. 6, pp. 127–68.

FRIED, R., and MAYER, M. F. (1948), 'Socio-emotional factors accounting for growth failure in children living in an institution', *J. Pediat.*, vol. 33, pp. 444–56.

FRIEDLANDER, B. Z. (1971), 'Listening, language and the auditory environment: automated evaluation and intervention', in J. Hellmuth (ed.) *The Exceptional Infant: II. Studies in Abnormalities*, Brunner/Mazel.

FURCHNER, C. S., and HARLOW, H. F. (1969), 'Preference for various surrogate surfaces among infant rhesus monkeys', *Psychonom, Sci.*, vol. 17, pp. 279–80.

GANZ, L. (1968), 'An analysis of generalization behavior in the stimulas-deprived organism', in G. Newton and S. Levine (eds.), *Early Experience and Behavior*, C. C. Thomas.

GARDNER, D. B., HAWKES, G. R., and BURCHINAL, L. G. (1961), 'Non-continuous mothering in infancy and development in later childhood', *Child Devel.*, vol. 32, pp. 225–34.

GARDNER, E. L., and GARDNER, E. B. (1970), 'Orientation of infant macaques to facially distinct surrogate mothers', *Devel. Psychol.*, vol. 3, pp. 409-10.

GARDNER, R. A., and GARDNER, B. T. (1969), 'Teaching sign language to a chimpanzee', *Science*, vol. 165, pp. 664–72.

GARROW, J. S., and PIKE, M. C. (1967), 'The long-term prognosis of severe infantile malnutrition', *Lancet*, vol. 1, pp. 1–4.

GARVIN, J. B., and SACKS, L. S. (1963), 'Growth potential of pre-school-aged children in institutional care: a positive approach to a negative condition', *Amer. J. Orthopsychiat.*, vol. 33, pp. 399–408.

GAW, F. (1925), 'A study of performance tests', *Brit. J. Psychol.*, vol. 15, pp. 374–92.

GEWIRTZ, J. L. (1968), 'The role of stimulation in models for child development', in L. L. Dittman (ed.), *Early Child Care: The New Perspectives*, Atherton Press.

GEWIRTZ, J. L. (1969), 'Mechanisms of social learning: some roles of stimulation and behavior in early human development', in D. A. Goslin (ed.), *Handbook of Socialization Theory and Research*, Rand McNally.

GIBSON, H. B. (1969), 'Early delinquency in relation to broken homes', *J. child Psychol. Psychiat.*, vol. 10, pp. 195–204.

GLASS, H. B. (1954), 'The genetic aspects of adaptability', *Proc. Assn Res. Nerv. Ment. Dis.*, vol. 23, pp. 367–77.

GLUECK, S., and GLUECK, E. T. (1950), *Unravelling Juvenile Delinquency*, Commonwealth Fund, New York.

GLUECK, S., and GLUECK, E. T. (1962), *Family Environment and Delinquency*, Routledge & Kegan Paul.

GOLDFARB, W. (1943), 'Infant rearing and problem behavior',
Amer. J. Orthopsychiat., vol. 13, pp. 249–65.

GOLDFARB, W. (1945a), 'Psychological privation in infancy and
subsequent adjustment', *Amer. J. Orthosychiat.*, vol. 15, pp. 247–55.

GOLDFARB, W. (1945b), 'Effects of psychological deprivation in
infancy and subsequent stimulation', *Amer. J. Psychiat.*,
vol. 102, pp. 18–33.

GOLDFARB, W. (1947), 'Variations in adolescent adjustment of
institutionally reared children', *Amer. J. Orthopsychiat.*, vol. 17,
pp. 449–57.

GOLDFARB, W. (1955), 'Emotional and intellectual consequences of
psychologic deprivation in infancy: a revaluation', in
P. H. Hoch and J. Zubin (eds.) *Psychopathology of
Childhood*, Grune & Stratton.

GORDON, H. (1923). *Mental and Scholastic Tests among Retarded
Children*, Board of Education.

GRAHAM, P., and GEORGE, S. (1972), 'Children's response to
parental illness: individual differences', *J. psychosom. Res.*, in press.

GREGORY, I. (1965), 'Anterospective data following childhood loss
of a parent', *Arch. gen. Psychiat.*, vol. 13, pp. 110–20.

GUITON, P. (1966), 'Early experience and sexual object choice
in the brown leghorn', *Anim. Behav.*, vol. 14, pp. 534–8.

HANDEL, G. (ed.) (1968), *The Psychosocial Interior of the
Family: A Source Book for the Study of Whole Families*,
Allen & Unwin.

HARLOW, H. F. (1958), 'The nature of love', *Amer. Psychol.*
vol. 13, pp. 673–85.

HARLOW, H. F. (1961), 'The development of affectional patterns in
infant monkeys', in B. M. Foss (ed)., *Determinants of Infant
Behaviour*, vol. 1, Methuen.

HARLOW, H. F. (1963), 'The maternal affectional system', in
B. M. Foss (ed.), *Determinants of Infant Behaviour*, vol. 2,
Methuen.

HARLOW, H. F., and GRIFFIN, G. (1965), 'Induced mental and
social deficits in rhesus monkeys', in S. F. Osler and R. E. Cooke
(eds.), *The Biosocial Basis of Mental Retardation*,
Johns Hopkins Press.

HARLOW, H. F., and HARLOW, M. K. (1965), 'The affectional
systems', in A. D. Schrier, H. F. Harlow and F. Stollnitz (eds.),
Behavior of Non-Human Primates, vol. 2, Academic Press.

HARLOW, H. F., and HARLOW, M. K. (1969), 'Effects of various
mother–infant relationships on rhesus monkey behaviours', in
B. M. Foss (ed.), *Determinants of Infant Behaviour*, vol. 4, Methuen.

HARLOW, H. F., and HARLOW, M. K. (1970), 'Developmental
aspects of emotional behavior', in P. Black (ed.), *Physiological
Correlates of Emotion*, Academic Press.

HARLOW, H. F., and SUOMI, S. J. (1971), 'Social recovery by isolation reared monkeys', *Proc. Nat. Acad. Sci.*, vol. 68, pp. 1534–8.

HARLOW, H. F., and ZIMMERMANN, R. R. (1959), 'Affectional responses in the infant monkey', *Science*, vol. 130, pp. 421–32.

HARLOW, H. F., SCHLITZ, K. A., and HARLOW, M. K. (1969), 'Effects of social isolation on the learning performance of rhesus monkeys', in *Proc. Second Int. Congr. Primatol., Atlanta, Georgia*, vol. 1, S. Karger.

HARPER, L. V. (1971), 'The young as a source of stimuli controlling caretaker behaviour', *Devel. Psychol.*, vol. 4, pp. 73–88.

HARPER, P. A., and WIENER, G. (1965) '*Sequelae* of low birth weight', *Ann. Rev. Med.*, vol. 16, pp. 405–20.

HAYWOOD, C. (1967), 'Experiential factors in intellectual development: the concept of dynamic intelligence', in J. Zubin and G. A. Jervis (eds.), *Psychopathology of Mental Development*, Grune & Stratton.

HEBB, D. O. (1949), *The Organization of Behavior*, Wiley.

HEIN, A., and HELD, R. (1967), 'Dissociation of the visual placing response into elicited and guided components', *Science*, vol. 158, pp. 390–92.

HEINICKE, C. M., and WESTHEIMER, I. J. (1965), *Brief Separations*, Longman.

HELD, R., and BAUER, J. A. (1967), 'Visually guided reaching in infant monkeys after restricted rearing', *Science*, vol. 155, pp. 718–20.

HELD, R., and HEIN, A. (1963), 'Movement-produced stimulation in the development of visually guided behavior', *J. comp. physiol. Psychol.*, vol. 56, pp. 872–6.

HELFER, R. E., and KEMPE, C. H. (eds.) (1968), *The Battered Child*, University of Chicago Press.

HENDERSON, N. D. (1964), 'Behavioral effects of manipulation during different stages in the development of mice', *J. comp. physiol. Psychol.*, vol. 57, pp. 284–9.

HERTZIG, M. E., BIRCH, H. G., THOMAS, A., and MENDEZ, O. A. (1968), 'Class and ethnic differences in the responsiveness of pre-school children to cognitive demands', *Monogr. Soc. Res. Child Devel.*, vol. 33, no. 117.

HESS, R. D. (1970), 'Social class and ethnic influences on socialization', in P. H. Mussen (ed.), *Carmichael's Manual of Child Psychology*, 3rd. edn, Wiley.

HESS, R. D., and SHIPMAN, V. C. (1965), 'Early experience and the socialization of cognitive modes in children', *Child Devel.*, vol. 36, pp. 869–86.

HESS, R. D., and SHIPMAN, V. C. (1967), 'Cognitive elements in maternal behavior', in J. P. Hill (ed.), *Minnesota Symposia on Child Psychology*, vol. 1, University of Minnesota Press.

HILL, O. (1972), 'Childhood bereavement and adult psychiatric disturbance', *J. psychosom. Res.*, in press.

HINDE, R. A. (1970), *Animal Behavior*, 2nd edn, McGraw-Hill.

HINDE, R. A. (1972), 'Mother–infant separation in rhesus monkeys', *J. psychosom. Res.*, in press.

HINDE, R. A., and SPENCER-BOOTH, Y. (1967), 'The effect of social companions on mother–infant relations in rhesus monkeys', in D. Morris (ed.), *Primate Ethology*, Weidenfeld & Nicolson.

HINDE, R. A., and SPENCER-BOOTH, Y. (1970), 'Individual differences in the responses of rhesus monkeys to a period of separation from their mothers', *J. child Psychol. Psychiat.*, vol. 11, pp. 159–76.

HINDE, R. A., and SPENCER-BOOTH, Y. (1971a), 'Towards understanding individual differences in rhesus mother–infant interaction', *Anim. Behav.*, vol. 19, pp. 165–73.

HINDE, R. A., and SPENCER-BOOTH, Y. (1971b), 'Effects of brief separation from mother on rhesus monkeys', *Science*, vol. 173, pp. 111–18.

HOFFMAN, L. W. (1963), 'Research findings on the effects of maternal employment on the child', in F. I. Nye and L. W. Hoffman (eds.), *The Employed Mother in America*, Rand McNally.

HOWELLS, J. G. (1970), 'Fallacies in child care: I. That "separation" is synonymous with "deprivation"', *Acta Paedopsychiat.*, vol. 37, pp. 3–14.

HOWELLS, J. G., and LAYNG, J. (1955), 'Separation experiences and mental health: a statistical study', *Lancet*, vol. 2, pp. 285–8.

HUBEL, D. H., and WIESEL, T. N. (1965), 'Binocular interaction in striate cortex of kittens reared with artificial squint', *J. Neurophysiol* vol. 28, pp. 1041–59.

HYMOVITCH, B. (1952), 'The effects of experimental variations on problem solving in the rat', *J. comp. physiol. Psychol.*, vol. 45, pp. 313–21.

IGEL, G. J., and CALVIN, A. D. (1960), 'The development of affectional responses in infant dogs', *J. comp. physiol. Psychol.*, vol. 53, pp. 302–5.

ILLINGWORTH, R. S. (ed.) (1958), *Recent Advances in Cerebral Palsy*. Churchill.

ILLINGWORTH, R. S., and HOLT, K. S. (1955), 'Children in hospital: some observations on their reactions with special reference to daily visiting', *Lancet*, vol. 2, pp. 1257–62.

ILLSLEY, R., and KINCAID, J. C. (1963), 'Social correlations of perinatal mortality', in N. R. Butler and D. G. Bonham (eds.), *Perinatal Mortality*, Livingstone.

IRVINE, E. E. (1966), 'Children in kibbutzim: thirteen years after', *J. child Psychol. Psychiat.*, vol. 7, pp. 167–78.

JENSEN, A. R. (1969), 'How much can we boost I Q and scholastic achievement?', *Harv. educ. Rev.*, vol. 39, pp. 1–123.

JESSOR, R., and RICHARDSON, S. (1968), 'Psychosocial deprivation and personality development', in *Perspectives on Human Deprivation: Biological, Psychological and Sociological*, US Department of Health, Education and Welfare.

JOLLY, H. (1969), 'Play is work: the role of play for sick and healthy children', *Lancet*, vol. 2, pp. 487–8.

JONES, H. E. (1954), 'The environment and mental development', in L. Carmichael (ed.), *Manual of Child Psychology*, Wiley.

JONSSON, G. (1967), 'Delinquent boys, their parents and grandparents', *Acta Psychiat. Scand.*, vol. 43, suppl. 195.

KAGAN, J. (1965), 'Reflection impulsivity at reading ability in primary grade children', *Child Devel.*, vol. 36, pp. 609–28.

KAUFMAN, I. C., and ROSENBLUM, L. A. (1969a), 'The waning of the mother–infant bond in two species of macaque', in B. M. Foss (ed.), *Determinants of Infant Behaviour*, vol. 4, Methuen.

KAUFMAN, I. C., and ROSENBLUM, L. A. (1969b), 'Effects of separation from mother on the emotional behaviour of infant monkeys', *Ann. New York Acad. Sci.*, vol. 159, pp. 681–95.

KERR, G. R., CHAMOVE, A. S., and HARLOW, H. F. (1969), 'Environmental deprivation: its effect on the growth of infant monkeys', *J. Pediat.*, vol. 75, pp. 833–7.

KING, R. D., and RAYNES, N. V. (1968), 'An operational measure of inmate management in residential institutions', *Soc. Sci. Med.*, vol. 2, pp. 41–53.

KING, R. D., RAYNES, N. V., and TIZARD, J. (1971), *Patterns of Residential Care: Sociological Studies in Institutions for Handicapped Children*, Routledge & Kegan Paul.

KIRK, S. A. (1958), *Early Education of the Mentally Retarded: An Experimental Study*, University of Illinois Press.

KISSEL, S. (1965), 'Stress-reducing properties of social stimuli', *J. Person. soc. Psychol.*, vol. 2, pp. 378–84.

KLACKENBERG, G. (1956), 'Studies in maternal deprivation in infants' homes', *Acta Pediat. (Stockholm)*, vol. 45, pp. 1–12.

KLAUS, R. A., and GRAY, S. W. (1968), 'The Early Training Project for Disadvantaged Children: a report after five years', *Monogr. Soc. Res. Child Devel.*, vol. 33, no. 4.

KLINGHAMMER, E. (1967), 'Factors influencing choice of mate in altricial birds', in H. W. Stevenson, E. H. Hess and H. L. Rheingold (eds.), *Early Behavior: Comparative and Developmental Approaches*, Wiley.

KLINGHAMMER, E., and HESS, E. H. (1964), 'Imprinting in an altricial bird: the blond ring dove', *Science*, vol. 146, pp. 265–6.

KOHEN-RAZ, R. (1968), 'Mental and motor development of kibbutz institutionalized and home-reared infants in Israel', *Child Devel.*, vol. 39, pp. 489–504.

KORNER, A. F., CHUCK, B., and DONTCHOS, S. (1968), 'Organismic determinants of spontaneous oral behaviour in neonates', *Child Devel.*, vol. 39, pp. 1145–57.

KORNER, A. F., and GROBSTEIN, R. (1966), 'Visual alertness as related to soothing in neonates: implications for maternal stimulation at early deprivation', *Child Devel.*, vol. 37, pp. 867–76.

KREITMAN, N., COLLINS, J., NELSON, B., and TROOP, J. (1970), 'Neurosis and marital interaction: I. Personality and symptoms', *Brit. J. Psychiat.*, vol. 117, pp. 33–46.

KUSHLIK, A. (1968), 'Social problems of mental subnormality', in E. Miller (ed.), *Foundations of Child Psychiatry*, Pergamon.

LAWTON, D. (1968), *Social Class, Language and Education*, Routledge & Kegan Paul.

LEE, E. S. (1951), 'Negro intelligence and selective migration: a Philadelphia test of the Klineberg hypothesis', *Amer. soc. Rev.*, vol. 16, pp. 227–33.

LEVINE, S. (1962), 'The effects of infantile experience on adult behavior', in A. J. Bachrach (ed.), *Experimental Foundations of Clinical Psychology*, Basic Books.

LEVY, D. M. (1958), *Behavioral Analysis: Analysis of Clinical Observations of Behavior as Applied to Mother–Newborn Relationships*, C. C. Thomas.

LEWIS, H. (1954), *Deprived Children*, Oxford University Press.

LIDDELL, H. (1950), 'Some specific factors that modify tolerance for environmental stress', in *Life Stress and Bodily Disease*, Williams & Wilkins.

LINDSLEY, D., and RIESEN, A. (1968), 'Biological substrates of development and behavior', in *Perspectives on Human Deprivation: Biological, Psychological and Sociological*, US Department of Health, Education and Welfare.

LORENZ, K. Z. (1935), 'Der Kumpan in der Umwelt des Vogels', *J. Ornithol. Berlin*, vol. 83; reprinted in C. H. Schiller (ed.), *Instinctive Behaviour*, Methuen, 1957.

LYLE, J. G. (1959), 'The effect of an institution environment upon the verbal development of imbecile children: I. Verbal intelligence', *J. ment. Defic. Res.*, vol. 3, pp. 122–8.

LYLE, J. G. (1960), 'The effect of an institutional environment upon the verbal development of imbecile children: III. The Brooklands residential family unit', *J. ment. Defic. Res.*, vol. 4, pp. 14–23.

LYNN, D., and SAWREY, W. L. (1959), 'The effects of father-absence on Norwegian boys and girls', *J. abnorm. soc. Psychol.*, vol. 59, pp. 258–62.

McCANDLESS, B. R. (1964), 'Relation of environmental factors to intellectual functioning', in H. A. Stevens and R. Heber (eds.), *Mental Retardation: A Review of Research,* University of Chicago Press.

MAAS, H. S. (1963), 'The young adult adjustment of twenty wartime residential nursery children', *Child Welf.,* vol. 42, pp. 57–72.

MACCARTHY, D., and BOOTH, E. M. (1970), 'Parental rejection and stunting of growth', *J. psychosom. Res.,* vol. 14, pp. 259–65.

MACCARTHY, D., LINDSAY, M., and MORRIS, L. (1962), 'Children in hospital with mothers', *Lancet,* vol. 1, pp. 603–8.

McCLEARN, G. E. (1970), 'Genetic influences on behavior and development', in P. H. Mussen (ed.), *Carmichael's Manual of Child Psychology,* 3rd edn, Wiley.

MACCOBY, E., and MASTERS, J. C. (1970), 'Attachment and dependency', in P. H. Mussen (ed.), *Carmichael's Manual of Child Psychology,* 3rd edn, Wiley.

McCORD, W., and McCORD, J. (1959), *The Origins of Crime: A New Evaluation of the Cambridge–Somerville Youth Study,* Columbia University Press.

McDONALD, A. D. (1964), 'Intelligence in children of very low birth weight', *Brit. J. prev. soc. Med.,* vol. 18, pp. 59–74.

McDONALD, A. D. (1967), *Children of Very Low Birthweight,* Heinemann Medical.

McKINNEY, J. P., and KEELE, T. (1963), 'Effects of increased mothering on the behavior of severely retarded boys', *Amer. J. ment. Defic.,* vol. 67, pp. 556–62.

MAPSTONE, E. (1969), 'Children in care', *Concern,* vol. 3, pp. 23–8.

MARRIS, P. (1958), *Widows and Their Families,* Routledge & Kegan Paul.

MARSHALL, W. A. (1968), *Development of the Brain,* Oliver & Boyd.

MASON, M. K. (1942), ' Learning to speak after six and one-half years of silence', *J. speech hear. Dis.,* vol. 7, pp. 295–304.

MASON, W. A. (1960), 'Socially mediated reduction in emotional responses of young rhesus monkeys', *J. abnorm. soc. Psychol.,* vol. 60, pp. 100–104.

MASON, W. A. (1967), 'Motivational aspects of social responsiveness in young chimpanzees', in H. W. Stevenson, E. H. Hess and H. L. Rheingold (eds.), *Early Behavior: Comparative and Developmental Approaches,* Wiley.

MASON, W. A. (1968), 'Early social deprivation in the non-human primates: implications for human behavior', in D. C. Glass (ed.), *Environmental Influences,* Russell Sage Foundation, New York.

MASON, W. A., DAVENPORT, R. K., and MENZEL, E. W. (1968), 'Early experience and the social development of rhesus monkeys and chimpanzees', in G. Newton and S. Levine (eds.), *Early Experience and Behavior,* C. C. Thomas.

MEAD, M. (1962), 'A cultural anthropologist's approach to maternal deprivation', in *Deprivation of Maternal Care: A Reassessment of its Effects*, World Health Organization, Geneva.

MEIER, G. W., and McGEE, R. K. (1959), 'A re-evaluation of the effect of early perceptual experience on discrimination performance during adulthood', *J. comp. physiol. Psychol.*, vol. 52, pp. 390–95.

MELZACK, R. (1965), 'Effects of early experience on behavior: experimental and conceptual considerations', in P. H. Hoch and J. Zubin (eds.), *Psychopathology of Perception*, Grune & Stratton.

MELZACK, R., and SCOTT, T. H. (1957), 'The effects of early experience on the response to pain', *J. comp. physiol. Psychol.*, vol. 50, pp. 155–61.

MENZEL, E. W. (1964), 'Patterns of responsiveness in chimpanzees reared through infancy under conditions of environmental restrictions', *Psychol. Forsch.*, vol. 27, pp. 337–65.

MIĆIĆ, Z. (1962), 'Psychological stress in children in hospital', *Int. nurs. Rev.*, vol. 9, pp. 23–31.

MILLAR, S. (1968), *The Psychology of Play*, Penguin.

MILLER, L. (1969), 'Child rearing in the kibbutz', in J. G. Howells (ed.), *Modern Perspectives in International Child Psychiatry*, Oliver & Boyd.

MILLER, R. E., CAUL, W. E. and MIRSKY, I. A. (1971), 'Patterns of eating and drinking in socially isolated rhesus monkeys', *Physiol. Behav.*, vol. 7, pp. 127–35.

MISSAKIAN, E. A. (1969), 'Effects of social deprivation on the development of patterns of social behavior', *Proc. Second Int. Congr. Primatol. Atlanta, Georgia*, vol. 2, S. Karger.

MOORE, T. W. (1963), 'Effects on the children', in S. Yudkin and A. Holme (eds.), *Working Mothers and Their Children*, Michael Joseph.

MOORE, T. W. (1964), 'Children of full-time and part-time mothers', *Int. J. soc. Psychiat.*, special congress issue no. 2.

MORGAN, G. A., and RICCIUTI, H. N. (1969), 'Infants' responses to strangers during the first year', in B. M. Foss (ed.), *Determinants of Infant Behaviour*, vol. 4, Methuen.

MOSS, H. A. (1967), 'Sex, age and state as determinants of mother-infant interaction', *Merrill-Palmer Q.*, vol. 13, pp. 19–36.

NAESS, S. (1959), 'Mother–child separation and delinquency', *Brit. J. Delinq.*, vol. 10, pp. 22–35.

NAESS, S. (1962), 'Mother-separation and delinquency: further evidence', *Brit. J. Criminol.*, vol. 2, pp. 361–74.

NISBET, J. D. (1953a), 'Family environment and intelligence', *Eugen. Rev.*, vol. 45, pp. 31–40.

NISBET, J. D. (1953b), *Family Environment: A Direct Effect of Family Size on Intelligence*, Eugenics Society.

NISSEN, H. W., CHOW, K. L., and SEMMES, J. (1951), 'Effects of restricted opportunity for tactual, kinesthetic and manipulative experience on the behavior of a chimpanzee', *Amer. J. Psychol.*, vol. 64, pp. 485–507.

NYLANDER, I. (1960), 'Children of alcoholic fathers', *Acta Paediat.*, vol. 49, suppl. 121.

NYMAN, A. J. (1967), 'Problem solving in rats as a function of experience at different ages', *J. genet. Psychol.*, vol. 110, pp. 31–9.

O'CONNOR, N. (1956), 'The evidence for the permanently disturbing effects of mother–child separation', *Acta Psychol.*, vol. 12, pp. 174–91.

O'CONNOR, N. (1968), 'Children in restricted environments', in G. Newton and S. Levine (eds.), *Early Experience and Behavior*, C. C. Thomas.

O'CONNOR, N., and FRANKS, C. M. (1960), 'Childhood upbringing and other environmental factors', H. J. Eysenck (ed.), *Handbook of Abnormal Psychology*, Pitman.

OLEINICK, M. S., BAHN, A. K., EISENBERG, L., and LILIENFELD, A. M. (1966), 'Early socialization experiences and intrafamilial environment', *Arch. gen. Psychiat.*, vol. 15, p. 344.

ORLANSKY, H. (1949), 'Infant care and personality', *Psychol. Bull.*, vol. 46, pp. 1–48.

OTTERSTRÖM, E. (1946), 'Delinquency and children from bad homes', *Acta Paediat. Scand.*, vol. 33, suppl. 5.

PARKES, C. M. (1964), 'Recent bereavement as a cause of mental illness', *Brit. J. Psychiat.*, vol. 110, pp. 198–204.

PARKES, C. M. (1965), 'Bereavement and mental illness', *Brit. J. med. Psychol.*, vol. 38, pp. 1–26.

PASAMANICK, B., and KNOBLOCH, H. (1961), 'Epidemiologic studies on the complications of pregnancy and the birth process', in G. Caplan (ed.), *Prevention of Mental Disorder in Children*, Basic Books.

PATTON, R. G., and GARDNER, L. I. (1963), *Growth Failure in Maternal Deprivation*, C. C. Thomas.

PETERSON, D. R., BECKER, W. C., HELLMER, C. A., SHOEMAKER, D. J., and QUAY, H. C. (1959), 'Parental attitudes and child adjustment', *Child Devel.*, vol. 30, pp. 119–30.

POWELL, G. F., BRASEL, J. A., and BLIZZARD, R. M. (1967), 'Emotional deprivation and growth retardation simulating idiopathic hypopituitarism: I. Clinical evaluation of the syndrome', *New Eng. J. Med.*, vol. 276, pp. 1271–8.

POWELL, G. F., BRASEL, J. A., RAITI, S., and BLIZZARD, R. M. (1967), 'Emotional deprivation and growth retardation simulating idiopathic hypopituitarism: II. Endocrinologic evaluation of the syndrome', *New Eng. J. Med.*, vol. 276, pp. 1279–83.

PRECHTL, H. F. R. (1963), 'The mother–child interaction in babies with minimal brain damage', in B. M. Foss (ed.), *Determinants of Infant Behaviour*, vol. 2, Methuen.

PREMACK, D. (1971), 'Language in chimpanzee?', *Science*, vol. 172, pp. 808–22.

PRINGLE, M. L. K., and BOSSIO, V. (1958a), 'Intellectual, emotional and social development of deprived children', *Vita Humana*, vol. 1, pp. 66–92.

PRINGLE, M. L. K., and BOSSIO, V. (1958b), 'Language development and reading attainment of deprived children', *Vita Humana*, vol. 1, pp. 142–70.

PRINGLE, M. L. K., and BOSSIO, V. (1960), 'Early prolonged separations and emotional adjustment', *J. child Psychol. Psychiat.*, vol. 1, pp. 37–48.

PRINGLE, M. L. K., and CLIFFORD, L. (1962), 'Conditions associated with emotional maladjustment among children in care', *Educ. Rev.*, vol. 14, pp. 112–23.

PRINGLE, M. L. K., and TANNER, M. (1958), 'The effects of early deprivation on speech development', *Lang. Speech*, vol. 1, pp. 269–87.

PROVENCE, S., and LIPTON, R. C. (1962), *Infants in Institutions*, International Universities Press.

PRUGH, D. G., STAUB, E. M., SANDS, H. H., KIRSCHBAUM, R. L., and LENIHAN, E. A. (1953), 'A study of the emotional reactions of children and families to hospitalization and illness', *Amer. J. Orthopsychiat.*, vol. 23, pp. 70–106.

RHEINGOLD, H. L. (1956), 'The modification of social responsiveness in institutional babies', *Monogr. Soc. Res. Child Devel.*, vol. 21, suppl. 63.

RHEINGOLD, H. L. (1960), 'The measurement of maternal care', *Child Devel.*, vol. 31, pp. 565–75.

RHEINGOLD, H. L. (1961), 'The effect of environmental stimulation upon social and exploratory behaviour in the human infant', in B. M. Foss (ed.), *Determinants of Infant Behaviour*, vol. 1, Methuen.

RHEINGOLD, H. L. (1963), *Maternal Behavior in Mammals*, Wiley.

RHEINGOLD, H. L. (1969), 'The effect of a strange environment on the behaviour of infants', in B. M. Foss (ed.), *Determinants of Infant Behaviour*, vol. 4, Methuen.

RHEINGOLD, H. L., and BAYLEY, N. (1959), 'The later effects of an experimental modification of mothering', *Child Devel.*, vol. 30, pp. 363–72.

RHEINGOLD, H. L., and SAMUELS, H. R. (1969), 'Maintaining the positive behaviour of infants by increased stimulation', *Devel. Psychol.*, vol. 1, pp. 520–27.

RHEINGOLD, H. L., GEWIRTZ, J., and ROSS, H. (1959), 'Social conditioning of vocalizations in the infant', *J. comp. physiol. Psychol.*, vol. 52, pp. 68–73.

RIESEN, A. (1965), 'Effects of early deprivation of photic stimulation', in S. F. Osler and R. E. Cooke (eds.), *The Biosocial Basis of Mental Retardation*, Johns Hopkins Press.

ROBERTSON, J. (1952), *A Two Year Old Goes to Hospital* (16 mm sound film with guidebook), Tavistock Child Development Research Unit.

ROBERTSON, J. (1958), *Going to Hospital with Mother* (16 mm sound film with guidebook), Tavistock Child Development Research Unit.

ROBERTSON, J. (ed.) (1962), *Hospitals and Children: A Parent's-Eye View*, Gollancz.

ROBERTSON, J., and BOWLBY, J. (1952), 'Responses of young children to separation from their mothers', *Courr. Cent. Int. Enf.*, vol. 2, pp. 131–42.

ROBERTSON, J., and ROBERTSON, J. (1967), *Young Children in Brief Separation: I. Kate, Aged Two Years Five Months in Fostercare for Twenty-Seven Days*, Tavistock Child Development Research Unit.

ROBERTSON, J., and ROBERTSON, J. (1968a), *Young Children in Brief Separation: II. Jane, Aged Seventeen Months in Fostercare for Ten Days*, Tavistock Child Development Research Unit.

ROBERTSON, J., and ROBERTSON, J. (1968b), *Young Children in Brief Separation: III. John, Aged Seventeen Months Nine Days in a Residential Nursery*, Tavistock Child Development Research Unit.

ROBINS, L. N. (1966), *Deviant Children Grown Up*, Williams & Wilkins.

ROBINS, L. N. (1970), 'The adult development of the antisocial child', *Seminar Psychiat.*, vol. 2, pp. 420–34.

ROBINSON, W. P., and RACKSTRAW, S. J. (1967), 'Variations in mother's answers to children's questions as a function of social class, verbal intelligence test scores and sex', *Sociology*, vol. 1, pp. 259–76.

ROE, A., and BURKS, B. (1945), *Adult Adjustment of Foster Children of Alcoholic and Psychotic Parentage and the Influence of the Foster Home*, Yale University Alcoholic Studies.

ROGERS, C. M., and DAVENPORT, R. K. (1971), 'Intellectual performance of differentially reared chimpanzees: III. Oddity', *Amer. J. ment. Defic.*, vol. 75, pp. 526–30.

ROSANOFF, A. J., HANDY, L. M., and PLESSET, I. R. (1941), *The Etiology of Child Behavior Difficulties, Juvenile Delinquency and Adult Criminality, with Special Reference to Their Occurrence in Twins*, Department of Institutions, Sacremento.

ROSENBLUM, L. A. (1971a), 'Infant attachment in monkeys', in H. R. Schaffer (ed.), *The Origins of Human Social Relations*, Academic Press.

ROSENBLUM, L. A. (1971b), 'General discussion', in H. R. Schaffer (ed.), *The Origins of Human Social Relations*, Academic Press.

ROSENBLUM, L. A., and HARLOW, H. F. (1963), 'Approach–avoidance conflict in the mother-surrogate situation', *Psychol. Rep.*, vol. 12, pp. 83–5.

ROSENTHAL, R., and JACOBSON, L. F. (1968), *Pygmalion in the Classroom: Teacher Expectation and Pupils' Intellectual Development*, Holt, Rinehart & Winston.

ROSENZWEIG, M. R., BENNETT, E. L., and DIAMOND, M. C. (1967), 'Effects of differential environments on brain anatomy and brain chemistry', in J. Zubin and G. A. Jervis (eds.), *Psychopathology of Mental Development*, Grune & Stratton.

ROSENZWEIG, M. R., KRECH, D., BENNETT, E. L., and DIAMOND, M. C. (1968), 'Modifying brain chemistry and anatomy by enrichment or impoverishment of experience', in G. Newton and S. Levine (eds.), *Early Experience and Behavior*, C. C. Thomas.

ROSS, J. M., and SIMPSON, H. R. (1971), 'The National Survey of Health and Development: II. Rate of school progress between 8 and 15 years and between 15 and 18 years', *Brit. J. educ. Psychol.*, vol. 41, pp. 125–35.

ROUDINESCO, J., and APPELL, G. (1950), 'Les répercussions de la stabilization hospitalière sur le développement psychomoteur des jeunes enfants', *Semaine des Hôpitaux de Paris*, vol. 26, pp. 2271–3. Abstract in R. Dinnage and M. L. K. Pringle, *Residential Child Care: Facts and Fallacies*, Longman, 1967.

ROUDINESCO, J., and APPELL, G. (1951), 'De certains répercussions de la carence de soins maternels et de la vie en collectivité sur les enfants de 1 á 4 ans', *Bulletins et Mémoires de la Société Médicale des Hôpitaux de Paris*, vol. 67, pp. 106–20. Abstract in R. Dinnage and M. L. K. Pringle, *Residential Child Care: Facts and Fallacies*, Longman, 1967.

ROWNTREE, G. (1955), 'Early childhood in broken families', *Pop. Stud.*, vol. 8, pp. 247–63.

RUTTER, M. (1966), *Children of Sick Parents: An Environmental and Psychiatric Study*, Oxford University Press.

RUTTER, M. (1970), 'Sex differences in children's responses to family stress', in E. J. Anthony and C. M. Koupernik (eds.), *The Child in His Family*, Wiley.

RUTTER, M. (1971a), 'Parent–child separation: psychological effects on the children', *J. child Psychol. Psychiat.*, vol. 12, pp. 233–60.

RUTTER, M. (1971b), 'Normal psychosexual development', *J. child Psychol. Psychiat.*, vol. 11, pp. 259–83.

RUTTER, M. (1972a), 'Language retardation and psychological development', in M. Rutter and J. A. M. Martin (eds.), *Young Children with Delayed Speech*, Heinemann.

RUTTER, M. (1972b), 'Maternal deprivation reconsidered',
J. psychosom. Res., in press.

RUTTER, M., and BROWN, G. W. (1966), 'The reliability and validity
of measures of family life and relationships in families containing
a psychiatric patient', *Soc. Psychiat.*, vol. 1, pp. 38–53.

RUTTER, M., and MITTLER, P. (1972), 'Environmental influences
on language development', in M. Rutter and J. A. M. Martin
(eds.), *Young Children with Delayed Speech*, Heinemann.

RUTTER, M., GRAHAM, P., and YULE, W. (1970),
A Neuropsychiatric Study in Childhood, Heinemann.

RUTTER, M., KORN, S., and BIRCH, H. G. (1963), 'Genetic and
environmental factors in the development of "primary reaction
patterns"', *Brit. J. soc. clin. Psychol.*, vol. 2, pp. 161–73.

RUTTER, M., TIZARD, J., and WHITMORE, K. (eds.) (1970),
Education, Health and Behaviour, Longman.

RUTTER, M., BIRCH, H. G., THOMAS, A., and CHESS, S. (1964),
'Temperamental characteristics in infancy and the ater
development of behavioural disorders', *Brit. J. Psychiat.*, vol. 110,
pp. 651–61.

SACKETT, G. P. (1968), 'Abnormal behavior in laboratory-reared
rhesus monkeys', in M. W. Fox (ed.), *Abnormal Behavior in
Animals*, Saunders.

SAINSBURY, P. (1972), 'Moving house and psychiatric disorder',
J. psychosom. Res., in press.

SAYEGH, Y., and DENNIS, W. (1965), 'The effect of supplementary
experiences upon the behavioural development of infants in
institutions', *Child Devel.*, vol. 36, pp. 81–90.

SCARR, S. (1969), 'Social introversion–extraversion as a heritable
response', *Child Devel.*, vol. 40, pp. 823–32.

SCHAFFER, H. R. (1963), 'Some issues for research in the study of
attachment behaviour', in B. M. Foss (ed.), *Determinants of
Infant Behaviour*, vol. 2, Methuen.

SCHAFFER, H. R. (1965), 'Changes in developmental quotient under
two conditions of maternal separation', *Brit. J. soc. clin. Psychol.*,
vol. 4, pp. 39–46.

SCHAFFER, H. R. (1966), 'Activity level as a constitutional
determinant of infantile reaction to deprivation', *Child Devel.*,
vol. 37, pp. 595–602.

SCHAFFER, H. R. (1971), *The Growth of Sociability*, Penguin.

SCHAFFER, H. R., and CALLENDER, W. M. (1959), 'Psychological
effects of hospitalization in infancy', *Pediatrics*, vol. 24, pp. 528–39.

SCHAFFER, H. R., and EMERSON, P. E. (1964), 'The development
of social attachments in infancy', *Monogr. Soc. Res. Child Devel.*,
vol. 29, no. 94.

SCHAFFER, H. R., and EMERSON, P. E. (1968), 'The effects of experimentally administered stimulation on developmental quotients of infants', *Brit. J. soc. clin. Psychol.*, vol. 7, pp. 61–7.

SCOTT, J. P. (1963), 'The process of primary socialization in canine and human infants', *Monogr. Soc. Res. Child Devel.*, vol. 28, no. 85.

SCOTT, J. P., and FULLER, J. L. (1965), *Genetics of the Social Behavior of the Dog*, University of Chicago Press.

SCRIMSHAW, N. S., and GORDON, J. E. (1968), *Malnutrition, Learning and Behavior*, M I T Press.

SEARLE, L. V. (1949), 'The organization of hereditary maze-brightness and maze-dullness', *Genet. Psychol. Monogr.*, vol. 39, pp. 279–325.

SEARS, R. R., PINTLER, M., and SEARS, P. S. (1946), 'Effect of father separation on preschool children's doll play aggression', *Child Devel.*, vol. 17, pp. 219–43.

SEAY, B., ALEXANDER, B. K., and HARLOW, H. F. (1964), 'Maternal behavior of socially deprived rhesus monkeys', *J. abnorm. soc. Psychol.*, vol. 69, pp. 345–54.

SHEPHERD, M., OPPENHEIM, B., and MITCHELL, S. (1971), *Childhood Behaviour and Mental Health*, University of London Press.

SHIELDS, J. (1954), 'Personality differences and neurotic traits in normal twin schoolchildren', *Eugen. Rev.*, vol. 45, pp. 213–46.

SHIELDS, J. (1968), 'Psychiatric genetics', in M. Shepherd and D. L. Davies (eds.), *Studies in Psychiatry*, Oxford University Press.

SIDOWSKI, J. B. (1970), 'Altruism, helplessness and distress: effects of physical restraint on the social and play behaviors of infant monkeys', *Proc. Seventy-Eighth Ann. Conv. Amer. Psychol. Assn.*

SIEGEL, A. E., and HAAS, M. B. (1963), 'The working mother: a review of research', *Child Devel.*, vol. 34, pp. 513–42.

SILVER, H. K., and FINKELSTEIN, M. (1967), 'Deprivation dwarfism', *J. Pediat.*, vol. 70, pp. 317–24.

SKEELS, H. M. (1942), 'A study of the effects of differential stimulation on mentally retarded children: follow-up report', *Amer. J. ment. Def.*, vol. 46, pp. 340–50.

SKEELS, H. M. (1966), 'Adult status of children with contrasting early life experiences', *Monogr. Soc. Res. Child Devel.*, vol. 31.

SKEELS, H. M., and DYE, H. (1939), 'A study of the effects of differential stimulation on mentally retarded children', *Proc. Amer. Assn Ment. Def.*, vol. 44, pp. 114–36.

SKEELS, H. M., and FILLMORE, E. A. (1937), 'The mental development of children from underprivileged homes', *J. genet. Psychol.*, vol. 50, pp. 427–39.

SKEELS, H. M., and HARMS, I. (1948), 'Children with inferior social histories: their mental development in adoptive homes', *J. genet. Psychol.*, vol. 72, pp. 283–94.

SKEELS, H. M., UPDEGRAFF, R., WELLMAN, B. L., and
WILLIAMS, H. M. (1938), 'A study of environmental stimulation:
an orphanage preschool project', *Univ. Iowa Stud. child Welf.*,
vol. 15, no. 4.

SKINNER, A. E., and CASTLE, R. L. (1969), *78 Battered Children:
A Retrospective Study*, National Association for the Prevention
of Cruelty to Children.

SKODAK, M., and SKEELS, H. M. (1949), 'A final follow-up
study of one hundred adopted children', *J. genet. Psychol.*,
vol. 75, pp. 85–125.

SLUCKIN, W. (1970), *Early Learning in Man and Animal*,
Allen & Unwin.

SPENCER-BOOTH, Y. (1970), 'The relationships between mammalian
young and conspecifics other than mothers and peers: a review', in
Advances in the Study of Behavior, vol. 3, Academic Press.

SPENCER-BOOTH, Y., and HINDE, R. A. (1971a), 'Effects of 6 days'
separation from mother on 18 to 32-week-old rhesus monkeys',
Anim. Behav., vol. 19, pp. 174–91.

SPENCER-BOOTH, Y., and HINDE, R. A. (1971b), 'Effects of brief
separations from mothers during infancy on behavior of rhesus
monkeys 6 to 24 months later', *J. child Psychol. Psychiat.*, vol.12,
pp. 157–72.

SPIRO, M. E. (1958), *Children of the Kibbutz*,
Oxford University Press.

SPROTT, W. J. H., JEPHCOTT, A. P., and CARTER, M. P. (1955),
The Social Background of Delinquency, University of Nottingham.

STACEY, M., DEARDEN, R., PILL, R., and ROBINSON, D. (1970),
Hospitals, Children and Their Families: The Report of a Pilot Study,
Routledge & Kegan Paul.

STARR, R. H. (1971), 'Cognitive development in infancy: assessment,
acceleration and actualization', *Merrill-Palmer Q.*, vol. 17,
pp. 153–86.

STEDMAN, D. J., and EICHORN, D. H. (1964), 'A comparison of
the growth and development of institutionalized and home-reared
mongoloids during infancy and early childhood', *Amer. J. ment.
Def.*, vol. 69, pp. 391–401.

STEIN, Z. A., and KASSAB, H. (1970), 'Nutrition', in J. Wortis (ed.),
Mental Retardation, vol. 2, Grune & Stratton.

STEIN, Z. A., and SUSSER, M. (1966), 'Nocturnal enuresis as a
phenomenon of institutions', *Devel. Med. child Neurol.*, vol. 8,
pp. 677–85.

STEIN, Z. A., and SUSSER, M. (1967), 'The social dimensions of a
symptom', *Soc. Sci. Med.*, vol. 1, pp. 183–201.

STEIN, Z. A., and SUSSER, M. (1970), 'Mutability of intelligence and
epidemiology of mild mental retardation', *Rev. educ. Res.*, vol. 40,
pp. 29–67.

STEINSCHNEIDER, A. (1967), 'Developmental psychophysiology', in Y. Brackbill (ed.), *Infancy and Early Childhood*, Free Press.

STEVENSON, I. (1957), 'Is the human personality more plastic in infancy and childhood?', *Amer. J. Psychiat.*, vol. 114, pp. 152–61.

STOLZ, L. M. (1960), 'Effects of maternal employment on children: evidence for research', *Child Devel.*, vol. 31, pp. 749–82.

STOLZ, L. M., et al. (1954), *Father Relations of War-Born Children*, Stanford University Press.

SUOMI, S. J., HARLOW, H. F., and DOMEK, C. J. (1970), 'Effect of repetitive infant–infant separation of young monkeys', *J. abnorm. Psychol.*, vol. 76, pp. 161–72.

TAIT, C. D., and HODGES, E. F. (1962), *Delinquents: Their Families and the Community*, C. C. Thomas.

TALBOT, N. B., SOBEL, E. H., BURKE, B. S., LINDEMANN, E., and KAUFMAN, S. B. (1947), 'Dwarfism in healthy children: its possible relation to emotional, nutritional and endocrine disturbances', *New Eng. J. Med.*, vol. 236, pp. 783–93.

THEIS, S. VAN S. (1924), *How Foster Children Turn Out*, State Charities Aid Association, New York.

THOMAS, A., CHESS, S., and BIRCH, H. G. (1968), *Temperament and Behaviour Disorders in Children*, University of London Press.

THOMAS, A., CHESS, S., BIRCH, H. G., HERTZIG, M., and KORN, S. (1963), *Behavioural Individuality in Early Childhood*, University of London Press.

THOMPSON, W. R., and GRUSEC, J. (1970), 'Studies of early experience', in P. H. Mussen (ed.), *Carmichael's Manual of Child Psychology*, 3rd edn, Wiley.

THOMPSON, W. R., and HERON, W. (1954), 'The effects of restricting early experience on the problem-solving capacity of dogs', *Canad. J. Psychol.*, vol. 8, pp. 17–31.

THOMPSON, W. R., and MELZACK, R. (1956), 'Early environment', *Sci. Amer.*, vol. 194, pp. 38–42.

THOMPSON, W. R., and OLIAN, S. (1961), 'Some effects on offspring behaviour of maternal adrenalin injection during pregnancy in three inbred mouse strains', *Psychol. Rep.*, vol. 8, pp. 87–90.

TIZARD, B. (1971), 'Environmental effects on language development: a study of residential nurseries', paper read at Annual Conference of the British Psychological Society, June 1971, University of Exeter.

TIZARD, B., and JOSEPH, A. (1970), 'Cognitive development of young children in residential care: a study of children aged 24 months', *J. child Psychol. Psychiat.*, vol. 11, pp. 177–86.

TIZARD, B., COOPERMAN, O., JOSEPH, A., and TIZARD, J. (1972), 'Environmental effects on language development: a study of young children in long-stay residential nurseries', *Child Devel.*, vol. 43.

TIZARD, J. (1964), *Community Services for the Mentally Handicapped*, Oxford University Press.

TIZARD, J. (1969), 'The role of social institutions in the causation, prevention and alleviation of mental retardation', in C. Haywood, (ed.), *Socio-Cultural Aspects of Mental Retardation*, Academic Press.

TIZARD, J., and TIZARD, B. (1971), 'The social development of two-year-old children in residential nurseries', in H. R. Schaffer (ed.), *The Origins of Human Social Relations*, Academic Press.

TIZARD, J., and TIZARD, B. (1972), 'The institution as an environment for development', in M. P. Richards (ed.), *The Integration of a Child into a Social World*, Cambridge University Press.

TODD, G. A., and PALMER, B. (1968), 'Social reinforcement of infant babbling', *Chil : Devel.*, vol. 39, pp. 591–6.

TRASLER, G. (1960), *In Place of Parents: A Study of Foster Care*, Routledge & Kegan Paul.

TURNER, C. H., DAVENPORT, R. K., and ROGERS, C. M. (1969), 'The effect of early deprivation on the soci behavior of adolescent chimpanzees', *Amer. J. Psychiat.*, vol. 125, pp. 1531–6.

UCKO, L. E. (1965), 'A comparative study of asphyxiated and non-asphyxiated boys from birth to five years', *Devel. Med. child Neurol.*, vol. 7, pp. 643–57.

VERNON, D. T. A., FOLEY, J. M., and SCHULMAN, J. L. (1967), 'Effect of mother–child separation and birth order on young children's responses to two potentially stressful experiences', *J. Person. soc. Psychol.*, vol. 5, pp. 162–74.

VERNON, D. T. A., FOLEY, J. M., SIPOWICZ, R. R., and SCHULMAN, J. L. (1965), *The Psychological Responses of Children to Hospitalization and Illness*, C. C. Thomas.

VERNON, P. E. (1969), *Intelligence and Cultural Environment*, Methuen.

WALTERS, R. H., and PARKE, R. D. (1965), 'The role of the distance receptors in the development of social responsiveness', in L. P. Lipsitt and C. C. Spiker (eds.), *Advances in Child Development and Behavior*, vol. 2, Academic Press.

WARDLE, C. J. (1961), 'Two generations of broken homes in the genesis of conduct and behaviour disorders in childhood', *Brit. med. J.*, vol. 2, pp. 349–54.

WATSON, P. (1970), 'How race affects IQ', *New Soc.*, 16 July, pp. 103–4.

WEISBERG, P. (1963), 'Social and nonsocial conditioning of infant vocalizations', *Child Devel.*, vol. 34, pp. 377–88.

WEST, D. J. (1969), *Present Conduct and Future Delinquency*, Heinemann.

WHEELER, L. R. (1942), 'A comparative study of the intelligence of East Tennessee mountain children', *J. educ. Psychol.*, vol. 33, pp. 321–34.

WHITE, B. L. (1967), 'An experimental approach to the effects of experience on early human behavior', in J. P. Hill (ed.), *Minnesota Symposia on Child Psychology*, vol. 1, University of Minnesota Press.

WHITE, B. L. (1971), *Human Infants: Experience and Psychological Development*, Prentice-Hall.

WHITTEN, C. F., PETTIT, M. G., and FISCHHOFF, J. (1969), 'Evidence that growth failure from maternal deprivation is secondary to undereating', *J. Amer. Med. Assn*, vol. 209, pp. 1675–82.

WHO EXPERT COMMITTEE ON MENTAL HEALTH (1951), *Report on the Second Session 1951*, World Health Organization, Geneva.

WIDDOWSON, E. M. (1951), 'Mental contentment and physical growth', *Lancet*, vol. 1, pp. 1316–18.

WIESEL, T. N., and HUBEL, D. H. (1963), 'Single cell responses in striate cortex of kittens deprived of vision in one eye', *J. Neurophsyiol.*, vol. 26, pp. 1003–17.

WIESEL, T. N., and HUBEL, D. H. (1965a), 'Comparison of the effects of unilateral and bilateral eye closure on cortical unit responses in kittens', *J. Neurophysiol.*, vol. 28, pp. 1029–40.

WIESEL, T. N., and HUBEL, D. H. (1965b), 'Extent of recovery from the effects of visual deprivation in kittens', *J. Neurophysiol.*, vol. 28, pp. 1060–72.

WOLFF, S., and ACTON, W. P. (1968), 'Characteristics of parents of disturbed children', *Brit. J. Psychiat.*, vol. 114, pp. 593–601.

WOLFHEIM, J. H., JENSEN, G. D., and BOBBITT, R. A. (1970), 'Effects of group environment on the mother–infant relationship in pig-tailed monkeys (*Macaca nemestrina*)', *Primates*, vol. 11, pp. 119–24.

WOLKIND, S. (1971), 'Children in care: a psychiatric study', thesis submitted for M.D., University of London.

WOODS, P. J., RUCKELSHAUS, S. I., and BOWLING, D. M. (1960), 'Some effects of "free" and "restricted" environmental rearing conditions upon adult behavior in the rat', *Psychol. Rep.*, vol. 6, pp. 191–200.

WOOTTON, B. (1959), *Social Science and Social Pathology*, Allen & Unwin.

WOOTTON, B. (1962), 'A social scientist's approach to maternal deprivation', in *Deprivation of Maternal Care: A Reassessment of its Effects*, World Health Organization, Geneva.

WORTIS, H. (1970), 'Poverty and retardation: social aspects', in J. Wortis (ed.), *Mental Retardation*, vol. 1, Grune & Stratton.

YANDO, R. M., and KAGAN, J. (1968), 'The effect of teacher tempo on the child', *Child Devel.*, vol. 39, pp. 27–34.

YARROW, L. J. (1961), 'Maternal deprivation: toward an empirical and conceptual re-evaluation', *Psychol. Bull.*, vol. 58, pp. 459–90.

YARROW, L. J. (1963), 'Research in dimensions of early maternal care', *Merrill-Palmer Q.*, vol. 9, pp. 101–14.

YARROW, L. J. (1964), 'Separation from parents during early childhood', in M. L. Hoffman and L. W. Hoffman (eds.), *Review of Child Development Research*, vol. 1, Russell Sage Foundation, New York.

YARROW, L. J. (1968), 'The crucial nature of early experience', in D. C. Glass (ed.), *Environmental Influences*, Russell Sage Foundation, New York.

YUDKIN, S., and HOLME, A. (1963), *Working Mothers and Their Children*, Michael Joseph.

YULE, W., and RAYNES, N. V. (1972), 'Behavioural characteristics of children in residential care: I. In relation to indices of separation', *J. child Psychol. Psychiat.*, in press.

ZIGLER, E. (1966), 'Mental retardation: current issues and approaches', in M. L. Hoffman and L. W. Hoffman (eds.), *Review of Child Development Research*, vol. 2, Russell Sage Foundation, New York.

Author Index

Subject Index